Tales of and about Jewish Youth during the *Fin-de-siécle* Era

An Annotated Gazette for a Transitional Decade in Upstate New York

Lawrence M. Ginsburg

UNIVERISTY PRESS OF AMERICA,® INC.
Lanham • Boulder • New York • Toronto • Plymouth, UK

Copyright © 2010 by
University Press of America,® Inc.
4501 Forbes Boulevard
Suite 200
Lanham, Maryland 20706
UPA Acquisitions Department (301) 459-3366

Estover Road
Plymouth PL6 7PY
United Kingdom

All rights reserved
British Library Cataloging in Publication Information Available

Library of Congress Control Number: 2009933243
ISBN: 978-0-7618-4865-3 (paperback : alk. paper)
eISBN: 978-0-7618-4866-0

Contents

List of Illustrations	v
Acknowledgments	vii
Part A	1
Straddling Latitude 43° North	1
A "Thumb Nail" Sketch of 19th-century Jewish Activism in Upstate New York Before the *Fin-de-siécle* Decade	2
Part B	5
A Jewish Orphanage	5
The Jewish Tidings	11
Betwixt and Between	13
Part C	14
Pre-Adolescent Truants or Rascal Lads	14
"Willie Provol, the Syracuse Match Peddler, Arrested for Looting Jamesville Carpenter Shop"	14
Erie Canal Circus-Boat Performer and *Cayuga Lake* Steam-Boat Concessionaire	17
Other Adolescent Activities	22
Early Adulthood Pursuits	24

Part D	26
Syracuse's *Der Rabbiner*	26
M. Peissackwotch = 'The Passover-Watcher' = '*Herr M*'	28
The Kier Brothers	28
Part E	30
Young Men's Hebrew Associations	30
Jewish Chautauqua Society	31
College-based Organizations	33
U.S.S. Olympia	34
Ripening of Ecumenical Dialogue	37
Part F	38
The *Fresh Air Fund*	38
A Model *Non*-Sectarian Entity	41
A Repentant Son?	46
The *Republic's* 'Color-Blind' Character	49
Part G	50
Epilogue	50
Notes	53
Appendix 1 "Daddy's Prophecy"	59
Appendix 2 October 9, 1899 letter from Richard Feinberg to William R. George	61
Appendix 3 Glossary	63
Bibliography	65
About the Author	69

Illustrations

Both the Roman Numerals and Captions appearing beneath *Figures I–II & V–XIII* have been inserted *de novo* by author. He also inserted the Roman Numerals appearing to the left of *Figures III–IV & XIV–XXV*. The remaining Captions have been replicated exactly as published within the respective texts authored by I. M. Brickner (*Figure III*), C. Adler (*Figure IV*) and J. R. Commons (*Figures XIV–XXV*). Other information bracketed below is specific to the corresponding pagination in the appended Bibliography where each contribution has been duly acknowledged.

Fig. I. Replica of face-side of official New York State flag inscribed in gold "Presented to 149th Reg't. N.Y.S.V." (top) *"by the JEWISH LADIES OF SYRACUSE, N.Y. Sep. 1862"* (bottom) [courtesy of 149th *New York State Volunteer Infantry Regiment Re-enactors,* a unit of the "North-South Skirmish Association"]   3

Fig. II. "An Appeal on Behalf of the Hebrew Sheltering Society of New York Orphan Asylum" [Composite of selected pages from publication belonging to author]   6

Fig. III. Jewish orphan asylum—Rochester, N. Y. [Replica of photograph appearing in treatise by I. M. Brickner (1912)]   8

Fig. IV. Louis Marshall at Syracuse [(Courtesy of Peter H. Schweitzer); Replica of photograph appearing in treatise by C. Adler (1931)]   10

Fig. V. Colonel Joseph Bondy   15

Fig. VI. Cohen's Big Canal Store [Artist Van Vliet's 1952 rendition of a photographed scene of unknown vintage archived at the *Onondaga Historical Association Museum and Research* Center]   18

Fig. VII. Sig Sautelle's Circus Canal Boat: "The BELLE"   20

Fig. VIII. Cayuga Lake Hotel [Etching by unknown artist portraying hotel and landing with the lake steamer *"The ISABEL"* at dock in Sheldrake, N. Y. (Courtesy of *The History Center in Tompkins County*)]   21

Fig. IX. Rev. Max Wechsler with his Hebrew class in 1899 [Earlier class than one taught by Rev. Jacob Levy that 'Willie' attended]   23

Fig. X. Board of Trustees of Temple Society of Concord [Seated from left to right, Benjamin Bronner, William Henochsberg & Adolph Guttman; standing from left to right, August Falker, Lee Schoener, Gates Thalheimer & David Danziger (Courtesy of *Temple Society of Concord*)]   27

Fig. XI. Y.M.H.A. (left); *Marshall Home* (right)   31

Fig. XII. A Publication of the Jewish Chautauqua Society [addendum to text of *Kiddush or Sabbath Sentiment in Home* by Dr. Henry Berkowitz (1898)]   32

Fig. XIII. Apprentice signal boy Samuel Ferguson (top far left) [Others standing with Commodore George Dewey, second from right on bridge of *U.S.S. Olympia* at the *Battle of Manila Bay* on May 1, 1898 were Marine orderly John H. McDougall & Chief Yeoman Merrick W. Creagh at far right (Courtesy of *Naval Historical Center*)]   35

Fig. XIV. Hotel, assembly hall, court house and jail, residence of Mr. George [p. 285]   38

Fig. XV. The original "Residents"—Winter of 1895–96 ("Daddy" top right) [p. 293]   39

Fig. XVI. A minor—10 YEARS OF AGE [p. 448]   40

Fig. XVII. Charley and his guardian [p. 439]   40

Fig. XVIII. "Aristocrats" [p. 287]   41

Fig. XIX. Officers of the battalion [p. 442]   42

Fig. XX. Baseball nine ("Daddy" top) [p. 445]   42

Fig. XXI. The laundry [p. 295]   43

Fig. XXII. Sewing class   44

Fig. XXIII. Chief of police [p. 441]   46

Fig. XXIV. A pauper [p. 288]   47

Fig. XXV. "Neverworks" (p. 291]   48

Acknowledgments

The author is grateful to Archivists at *Cornell University, Syracuse University* and *YIVO* for their assistance. He admittedly still has a lot to learn about stilted grammar. Plaudits are due Rachel E. Wintner for diplomatically rescuing him from many of his abuses of 'good English' conventions as may still stick out through no fault of her own. Likewise, he is especially indebted to Sybil A. Ginsburg, M.D. his wife, for her support and encouragement.

438 Snug Harbor
DeRuyter, NY 13052

Part A

STRADDLING LATITUDE 43° NORTH

Preliminary to the construction of the *Erie Canal*, early surveyors of what became known as the "Big Ditch" or "Governor Clinton's Folly" were looking across terrain in an easterly-westerly direction reaching from Central New York toward *Lake Erie*. Rolling bluffs and gravel-rich promontories deposited during the Ice Age had to be surmounted since the resulting route was 168 feet higher in altitude at Buffalo than at Syracuse. It traversed glacially up-heaved escarpments as well as the soggy Montezuma Marshes. Towpaths for "packet-boat" mule-pulling teams soon lined the waterway.

    A system of "feeder canals" was dug to connect *Lake Ontario* to the north with the so-called "Finger Lakes" to the south. The identity of "Hiawatha" (*i.e.*, Chief of the *Onondaga Tribe* and founder of the *Iroquois Indian Confederacy*) was commandeered by Henry Wadsworth Longfellow and removed to the mid-west in his epic poem. Hiawatha reputedly likened the Finger Lakes to the imprint of one's hand pressed against "Mother Earth" (*i.e.*, with the thumb representative of *Oneida Lake* while several such as the Seneca, Cayuga, Onondaga and Mohawk bodies of water, were named after other nearby tribal constituencies). Ancient Native American legends likewise account for the salinity of *Onondaga Lake*'s briny-water—dubbing Syracuse as the "Salt City"—before geologists became cognizant of the accumulations of thick salt remaining from the *Late Silurian* period.

    Meteorologists have characterized Arctic winds with their accompanying precipitation as they sweep across the "Great Lakes" and Finger Lakes as the "Lake Effect." The resulting snowdrifts invariably blanket the Buffalo, Rochester, Syracuse and Utica metropolitan areas. The easterly-westerly *Erie Canal* coupled with the auxiliary network of Finger Lakes—each of which stretches for many miles along a southerly-northerly axis—are frozen to navigable commercial traffic during the winter months of each year.

A "THUMB NAIL" SKETCH OF 19TH-CENTURY JEWISH ACTIVISM IN UPSTATE NEW YORK BEFORE THE *FIN-DE-SIÉCLE* DECADE

Mordecai Manuel Noah was among the most influential Jews in the early 19th-century United States. As an ardent utopian Zionist, he helped purchase a tract of land in 1825 on Grand Island along the *Niagara River* near the northwestern corner of New York State where he envisioned the creation of a Jewish colony called "Ararat."[1] His proposed plan, while eliciting interest and discussion, proved to be a disappointment. Noah came to realize that Palestine was the only available recourse for the establishment of such Jewish settlements. He lectured and wrote about the need for such a homeland until his death in 1851.

To the west of Syracuse, the *Book of Mormon* had been revealed to Joseph Smith in Palmyra. To the east, a religious society of "Perfectionists" known as the *Oneida Community* took root. Their members originally held all property in common and practiced complex marriage arrangements. Provision for the collective care of children was relegated to a system not unlike what would emerge a half-century later in many an Israeli *kibbutz*.

A diverse array of human rights activists and utopian idealists contributed to a rich ferment of social consciousness in 19th-century upstate New York. They included numerous Jewish men and women. The women's suffragist movement was one such force. Among the participants was Ernestine L. Rose, an internationally known feminist, who came to Syracuse and delivered an impassioned plea for equal rights for women at the *Third National Women's Rights Convention* (attended by 2,000 people). In her address to the assembly (1852), she introduced herself as "a daughter of poor crushed Poland, and the downtrodden and persecuted people called the Jews, 'a child of Israel' . . . " (p. 326).

As early as March 14, 1855, enough establishments had been originated in the central business district of Syracuse for the commercial enclave to be dubbed "Jerusalem" (Ginsburg, 2001). Two years later, a local newspaper felt justified in publishing the following observation:

> "We notice that a number of dry good merchants . . . are preparing to remove their goods to the new stores on South Salina Street. According to present appearances, Jerusalem will be left in almost undisputed possession of that old and still very desirable locality for trade" (p. 4).

Meanwhile, abolitionists continued their *ante-bellum* activities in furnishing 'way-stations' along the "underground railroad" for escaped slaves fleeing northward to the nearby Canadian provinces. Frederick Douglass of Rochester and Harriet Tubman of Auburn were among the Southern-born who eventually settled in upstate New York.

During the *Civil War* in Central New York, the Jewish community of Syracuse sponsored the formation of Company A of the *149th Regiment of the New York State Volunteers.* Not only was a complement of young adults and men raised under communal auspices to fight for the Northern cause; but, by September of 1862 the "Jewish Ladies of Syracuse, N.Y." had fabricated and presented a battle flag *(Fig. I)*. Elsewhere, a fuller account of the unit's war service has been published (Ginsburg, 2001).

The bloody savagery of Russian *anti-*Semitism provided an impetus to those seeking a refuge in North America from what internationally became

Fig. I. Replica of face-side of official New York State flag inscribed in gold "Presented to 149th Reg't. N.Y.S.V." (top) "by the JEWISH LADIES OF SYRACUSE, N.Y. Sep. 1862" (bottom) [courtesy of 149th New York State Volunteer Infantry Regiment Re-enactors, a unit of the "North-South Skirmish Association"].

known as the "1881 Pogroms" (Learsi, 1954, pp. 124–136). Many such immigrants were from Middle and Eastern Europe; often, they already had been acclimated to life amidst harsh-weather "snow-belts." Paved roads, department stores and mail order houses had not yet penetrated the remote reaches of the interior American countryside. During the *pre*-turn-of-the-century "Gay Nineties," the "horse-less" carriage, the radio and the telephone were not as yet relegated to the realm of futuristic dreams.

W. Lee Provol (*i.e.,* the formal name under which he later became known) reminisced in his autobiographical memoir entitled *The Pack Peddler* (1933):

"Many a cold winter morning I helped Dad to the railway station, drawing his packs on my sled. Upon arriving at his destination he would strap the packs on his back and carry a valise (as they were called in those days) in each hand. Aside from being loaded with these heavy packs, he wore a heavy woolen-lined leather jacket, with corduroy trousers, the bottoms of which were tucked into large leather boots . . . No man worked harder than these pack peddlers. The peddler in those days was the farmer's department store. People looked forward to his visits for their supplies . . . These sturdy men would travel miles a day over rough, dusty roads, in sunshine, rain storms, and heavy snow storms in winter. In each farmhouse the peddler would unpack his merchandise and display it all over the room . . . When the peddler had all his merchandise on display, the entire family including the farm help, would gather around and select the things they wanted to buy. If the peddler did not have what the farmers wanted, it was placed on order to be delivered on his next trip . . . When the day's work was done and dusk hovered over the sky, the peddler would stop at some farmhouse to put up for the night. He usually exchanged merchandise for his supper, night's lodging, and breakfast . . . The children especially enjoyed having the peddler as guest. He would tell them stories of other boys and girls in foreign lands and the cities nearby . . . " (pp. 18–21).

Settlers for generations beforehand had been attracted to the undulating countryside. Apples grown upon the hilly terrain trod by pioneers, like the storied 'Johnnie Appleseed,' were available for picking. Other fruit orchards lined the shores of the nearby Finger Lakes whose late spring frosts impeded their buds from premature blossoming. Harvested hops were regularly transported to breweries situated alongside the *Erie Canal*. Locally caught species of fresh fish were available; meat was smoked for future use. Sprinkled sawdust enveloped slabs of lake or pond frozen ice were used by dairy farmers in the 'hinterlands' so that they could ship milk to more distant consumers *via* the growing network of railroads. Vegetable surpluses were stored in cold cellars. Itinerant peddlers with horses and wagons were equipped to acquire such transient 'foodstuffs' not only for their own families; but also, for marketing to other customers.

Part B

A JEWISH ORPHANAGE

Charitable endeavors by various communal organizations known as "Sheltering Societies" had been functioning in locales throughout the state during the last quarter of the 19th-century. Among them were certain Jewish-oriented orphanages. They had been founded to provide custodial havens for "parent-absent" or "guardian-less" youths. It is apt to note the retrospective account of Matthew A. Crenson (1998):

> " . . . By the 1890s, one out of every hundred children in the state was living in an orphanage; in New York City, the rate was one in thirty-five. It was the orphan capital of the United States" (pp. 49–50).

The *Hebrew Sheltering Guardian Society of New York* was one such institution. It was founded in 1879—pursuant to its 'Mission Statement'—"for the purpose of providing a Jewish home and a Jewish up-bringing for neglected, destitute and orphaned Jewish children." The President of the institution's Board of Management in 1900 noted that "by far the greater number" of the children housed at the Grand Boulevard (*i.e.,* 150th to 151st Streets) premises were not only " . . . *deserted* or *destitute* . . . foreign born . . . "; but, also " . . . half orphans . . . " (Levy, 1900, pp. 5–7). An Appeal for funding (*Fig. II*) is excerpted from a typical annual drive:

> "We ardently desire to give every boy and girl we rear a certain amount of elementary technical training, so that they may be able to turn their hands to useful and productive labor. It is important to encourage this, and so to wean them from the tendency to 'dealing' and 'peddling,' which is almost hereditary with them . . . " (*op. cit.,* p. 13).

An Appeal

On behalf of the..... **Hebrew Sheltering Guardian Society** of New York

Orphan Asylum

Grand Boulevard, 150th to 151st Sts., New York.

THE Hebrew Sheltering Guardian Society of New York was founded twenty-one years ago for the purpose of providing a Jewish home and a Jewish up-bringing for neglected, destitute and orphaned Jewish children.

The motto adopted by the Society—

"Shelter us under the Shadow of Thy Wings"

—indicates the spirit in which the founders approached their task, and which has pervaded our thoughts and directed our acts ever since.

3

Board of Managers.

SAMUEL D. LEVY, President.
(Vacant) First Vice-President.
Mrs. DR. S. TELLER, 2d Vice-Pres't.
ELY BERNAYS, Treasurer.
GUSTAVE ECKSTEIN, Hon. Sec.

SAM'L S. ROSENSTAMM,
Mrs. CLARA JACOBS,
Mrs. CECELIA ROSETT,
Mrs. L. HESS,
Mrs. J. ROSENFELD,
Mrs. A. FALCK,
Mrs. M. GOODHART.

Number of Children in the Home on October 1, 1900:

Boys............................ 534
Girls............................ 373
                                  —— 907

Orphans........................ 37
Half-orphans................... 406
Deserted children.............. 247
Destitute...................... 217
                                  —— 907

There have been 4156 Children in this Institution since its foundation. Of these

1702 were born in the United States,
163   "   "   "   Great Britain,
2202 "   "   "   European Countries, not English-speaking.

Receipts from all sources in 1899-1900..$102,164.76
Total Expenditure........................ 102,097.52

Balance in hand of Treasurer $67.24

Fig. II. "An Appeal on Behalf of the Hebrew Sheltering Society of New York Orphan Asylum" [Composite of selected pages from publication belonging to author].

Another such 19th-century Jewish orphanage—beyond the confines of New York City—was situated in Rochester. As early as 1877, the *Jewish Orphan Asylum of Western New York*[1] was chartered "to provide shelter and upbringing for the orphans of Jewish parents." In 1884 (*Fig. III*), it was located at a midpoint between Buffalo and Syracuse, in a large house with ample grounds along the *Genesee River* gorge at North Saint Paul Street in Rochester.

In the words of Ida Klein Richardson (1938), a Rochester historian:

"Dependent Jewish children from five to twelve years of age were admitted to the institution. Admissions were made through application to the Emergency Committee of the organization. The children were committed to the orphanage by the poor law official of the city in which they resided. The institution complied with the rules of the State Board of Charities" (pp. 15–16).

Further institutional rules provided as follows:

"No inmate of the Asylum shall be discharged except by a majority vote of the Board of Trustees. Within three months before each annual meeting of the Executive Board, a list of the inmates of the asylum who shall attain the age of sixteen years during the ensuing year shall be forwarded to each member of the Board; thereupon, at such meeting, a resolution shall be passed for the dismissal of such orphans upon reaching that age, unless good cause be shown for further detention, in which event special provision shall be made for further care and custody. Upon the passage of a resolution of dismissal, the child shall be returned to the local society of the particular city from which the orphan has been sent, to find employment, or to otherwise care for the same"

The Jewish Tidings, a Rochester weekly journal, opined on August 8, 1890 that the limit for the departure of wards from the *Orphan Asylum* should be increased to eighteen years of age. Far from admitting the newspaper's charge that a young woman remaining under the asylum's custody had been "sent out at a tender age to seek her own living," a rejoinder by one of the institution's Directors illustrated the circumstances which attended the Board's determination that she had not been "fit to be an inmate of our institution" (Landsberg, p. 7). Although over sixteen years old at the time, he (1890) wrote:

" . . . we had not yet adopted any rule fixing a certain age for the discharge of children" (*ibid.*). Alternate arrangements were facilitated in her behalf including room and board, constant supervision and instruction in tailoring until "suddenly, when she was about eighteen years old, she went to New York without our permission and thus escaped entirely from our control . . . " (*ibid.*).

Other published sentiments, expressing praise for earlier care and supervision at the orphanage, were written by the young poetess Jenny Jacobs (1889 &

Fig. III. Jewish orphan asylum—Rochester, N. Y. [Replica of photograph appearing in treatise by I. M. Brickner (1912)]

1890). Similar tributes by former inmates and their adoptive parents were likewise recorded.

Richardson (1938), a long-time employee of the *Orphan Asylum,* wrote that a woman "known to have been among the first group" to reside upon its original grounds "admitted that life . . . was much as it would have been in a private home" (*ibid.,* p. 16). She outlived the tolling of the Common Era's 2nd *millennium* by several decades. In her account, as related to Richardson:

> "Downstairs was a long bare looking playroom with individual cupboards for each child's toys. A large dining room and kitchen as well as the superintendent's office and some of his living rooms were on the ground floor. On the second floor were the sleeping quarters. There were two dormitories—one for the girls and one for the boys. In the front of the house was a very large yard with spreading trees in it, in the rear a fairly large playground with apparatus such as swings, see-saws, etc . . . .The superintendent's children mingled with the residents, and no distinction was made in the matter of clothing, in treatment, or in any other way. The children went together to the Temple services and Sunday School, and all attended No. 20 school, the public school nearest the orphanage. After school they were allowed to visit the children in the neighborhood. About five P.M. a large cow-bell of the type used in the country to being in the farm hands in for meals, was rung. Its loud clanging was the signal for the children to return for supper. After supper the children were confined to the grounds, but neighboring children were welcome to visit and play in the playground or recreation room until bedtime . . . " (*ibid.,* pp. 16–17).

The orphanage's "Board [was] always trying its utmost to keep with the trends in child care" as Richardson further noted:

> "A committee of women was appointed to purchase materials for the children's clothing. A seamstress was employed to make clothing for the girls and blouses for the boys, assisted by the girls. At the age of sixteen, the girls and boys were discharged from the orphanage to make their own way in the world" (*ibid.,* p. 18).

The *Orphan Asylum* served a dual purpose in attempting to propagate both Jewish and American values. It not only functioned to infuse vulnerable children—in the wake of a mass immigration—with middle class aspirations such as a primary school education; but, also tried to maintain the Jewish threads of their cultural identity.

An unidentified reporter for the *Rochester Sunday Times* had occasion to interview the *Orphan Asylum's* Superintendent and his Matron-wife. It was reprinted in the July 11, 1890 issue of the *Tidings*:

> "Any Jewish orphan boy or girl is admitted upon proper application to the executive board, provided they be between the ages of five and seventeen years.

No applicant within these limits has as yet been rejected . . . By a rigid rule of the asylum, all the children are compelled to attend public school which is in the vicinity. Religious instruction, especially Biblical history is given them at stated times by Dr. Landsberg. Max Moll teaches them to translate the Old Testament from the original Hebrew . . . (p. 8).

It is worth reexamining the declarative position of Louis Marshall[2]—a native-born Syracuse lawyer (*Fig. IV*) and representative at the seminal *tri*-city deliberations leading to the aforementioned *Orphan Asylum's* birth—shortly before the operative decade which is the subject of this study. In a paper subsequently read at the *Proceedings of the 5th National Conference of Jewish Charities*, the renowned New York City civil rights lawyer argued that Judaism taught and practiced in Jewish child care institutions (*i.e.*, including settlement houses, orphanages and reformatories):

Fig. IV. Louis Marshall at Syracuse [(Courtesy of Peter H. Schweitzer); Replica of photograph appearing in treatise by C. Adler (1931)].

"... must not be a Judaism that is apologetic ... it must not be a Judaism in name only ... it must not be a Judaism of the sterilized ... variety" (1908, p. 116).

He called for intensified religious instruction and observance, including the teaching of Hebrew, in such institutions (*ibid.,* p. 119).

THE JEWISH TIDINGS

The above-captioned Rochester-based newspaper began publishing a weekly journal on February 5, 1887. The cost of a subscription was $2.00 *per annum.* Featured in most issues were communications from regular contributors in upstate New York's principal *tri*-cities, other State cities and locales as well as national and even international readership. Inquiries about advertising, subscriptions and news items were welcomed at regularly published mailing addresses throughout the United States, Glasgow, Liverpool, London and Trinidad. The publication's masthead, early in the 1890's, proclaimed: "This Paper has a larger Circulation than any other Jewish Publication in America!" By 1897, it no longer appeared in print.

Controversies about the sanctity of so-called "Sunday Laws" had long been a 'bone of contention' throughout the land. A preponderance of gentiles remained committed to maintaining the gentile Sabbath as the "Lord's Day of Rest." A nascent disdain had been looming, perhaps, against tolerant laws countenancing the weekend availability of alcoholic beverages and open-street "hucksterism." In Rochester, to cite a further example, a daily newspaper had already been pressured against continued publication of a Sunday edition.

In a Jewish context, the reigning editorial policy of the *Tidings,* as it popularly became known, continued to herald itself as "A Fearless Exponent of Progressive Judaism!" Three Syracuse subscribers, in the May 2, 1890 issue, voiced opinions about the proposition of supplementary religious services and/or lectures contemplating regular Sunday attendance beyond more traditional available options. From top to bottom on the front page, the captions in the *Tidings* introduced each discourse as follows:

(a) "AN EMINENT OPINION: A Syracuse Attorney Earnestly Favors the Proposition. Louis Marshall, Syracuse"
(b) "THE 'TIDINGS' IS RIGHT: So Says a Prominent Syracuse Physician. Dr. Henry L. Elsner, Syracuse"
(c) "SEES NO OBJECTION: Another Well-Known Physician on the Right Side. Dr. Nathan Jacobson, Syracuse"

A week later, a column in the *Tidings* written by "Rev. Dr. A. Guttman, Syracuse" began with the following sentence: "I am opposed to divine services on Sunday for Jews, not to Sunday lectures" (p. 1). To be clear, the debate did not break down clearly along 'progressive' and '*non*-progressive' lines. The following week, a letter to the editor authored by Syracusan Joseph Felker (1890) was published:

> "I am opposed to supplementary religious services on Sunday. I consider it an indirect attempt towards a change of the Sabbath to Sunday. I believe that the attendance at such services would be largely drawn from the Friday evening and Saturday worshippers. Services in three successive days every week can not reasonably be expected to be largely attended, besides giving us the opportunity of choosing 'the day' for our devotions, and what might prove successful to one would possibly be so at the expense of the other" (p. 1).

As a microcosm of the national furor, Syracuse Jewry had already begun to fragment among doctrinal lines. Opponents viewed the innovations first endorsed above as attempts to "stab the Jewish Sabbath in the back" and tantamount to heresy.

The *Tidings*—while trumpeting the slogan that "There is no Jewish race!"—seemed particularly offensive to Rochester's Russian/Polish Jewish citizens. "Scarcely a day passes that some vicious Polish Jew does not strike, stab or shoot another," according to repeated local accounts printed in the *Tidings*. The editorial on July 18, 1890 spoke for itself:

> "A barrier to the progress of the Russian Jews who constantly flock to this country is the filth in which some of them live. The *Tidings* feels a warm interest in the welfare of the poor, unfortunate Jews who are driven by persecution from their homes in Russia to find a haven of rest in this land of the free. These despised and downtrodden people have not kept pace with the German-American Jews in life's struggle. The great majority of Russian Jews in this country are poor and ignorant and are not permitted to associate with their more co-religionists. The lower quarter of this city is thronged with some of these people whose dirty and filthy habits of living are notorious. The squalor, in which they wallow, breeds disease and the *Tidings* desires to utter a timely note of warning. The summer's heat is now upon us and the unfortunate do not realize that cleanliness is essential to health and life should be impressed with this necessity. The *Tidings* appeals to the Board of Health of Rochester to adopt stringent measures whereby a reform in the direction named may be accomplished" (p. 4).

When a reporter for the *Tidings* wrote about a group picnic or outing at one of the "watering places" frequented by a "party of our representative people," it would have been safe to assume that prospective vacationers communicating in their Yiddish-inflectioned jargon, emanating from eastern Europe, were not among the invitees.

BETWIXT AND BETWEEN

At the beginning of the last decade of the 19th-century (*i.e.,* "The Gilded Age" in American jargon), Orthodox Jews in major cities of upstate New York were increasing their independence from the more established neighboring Reform congregations (Rudolph, *op. cit.,* pp. 129-133). The influx of orphans of East European parentage was beginning to supplant its predominantly German-Jewish brethren. In Syracuse, for example, a benefactor presented a major edifice "to be used as a Jewish orphan asylum, the one in Rochester being considered not *kosher* enough to satisfy the Orthodox element..." (*ibid.,* p. 170). Although we remain without enough statistical data about the diverse religious heritages involved to gauge reliable comparison percentages, it was becoming evident that 'mainstream' charitable organizations had to begin vying with one another for communal recognition.

The polarization was theologically manifested in the lingering 'Old World' rift between a few German-language oriented Jewish Seminaries (*Jüdisch-Theologisches Seminar*) and Yiddish-language oriented *Yeshivot*. In an American context, it often pitted a German/rabbinical liturgy *vis-à-vis* a Yiddish/Hebrew liturgy with English and *semi*-German/Russian modes of thought remaining as common denominators. Bertram W. Korn (1972), in *German-Jewish Intellectual Influences on American Jewish Life, 1824–1972,*[3] defined *"The 'Wissenschaft' Concept of Jewish Learning"* as an endeavor "to give intellectual validation to Judaism and Jewish history, hence also to the decision of individual Jews to remain loyal the Jewish heritage" (p. 7). According to one authority he cited, the works of '*Wissenschaft*' were expected to achieve high levels of "scholarly objectivity, broad scope, meaningful context, proper form and style and—respectability" (*ibid.*).

Korn (*op. cit.*) interpreted the modernistic novel of Chaim Potok, *The Chosen* (1967), to illustrate his thesis. It contrasts *inter*-generational as well as *intra*-generational struggles within and between particular 'brands' of "orthodox establishments" and a young man's quest to express his artistic talent while remaining loyal to his traditional values. Baseball metaphors were invoked to exemplify the underlying approaches to life. In Korn's analysis: "The difference between [the rivals' worlds]—the one influenced as much by German *Wissenschaft* as by the *Vilna Gaon*—is dramatized in Chaim Potok's exquisitely fashioned novel..." (p. 10).

Part C

PRE-ADOLESCENT TRUANTS OR RASCAL LADS

As soon as they were old enough to play with marbles, children often gathered old rags, bottles and scrap iron for their older brothers to barter for a penny or more. Others, from an early age, distributed advertising handbills in exchange for 'free' candy. Enterprising juveniles had already begun delivering newspapers before their headlines were even understood by them. "Hawking" peanuts and lemonade for concessionaires at vaudeville theatricals, traveling circus extravaganzas, regional agricultural fairs, revivalist meetings, political rallies and side-shows extolling various patent medicines were likewise financially rewarding.

Many a Jewish youngster began his commercial career by selling fruit and bananas purchased from a local wholesaler to 'greenhorn' Europeans, at refueling lay-overs between major stations, along the westbound routes of the *New York Central Railroad*. Surmounting such a foreigner's communication deficits might, in fact, have proven advantageous for a Jewish-American neophyte.

"WILLIE PROVOL, THE SYRACUSE MATCH PEDDLER, ARRESTED FOR LOOTING JAMESVILLE CARPENTER SHOP"

Joseph Bondy (*Fig. V*), a Syracuse lawyer, was retained by one Henry Provol to represent his aforementioned son "Willie," a juvenile match peddler who had been accused of robbery and put in jail. Colonel Bondy (1933), who attained his military rank during the first *World War*, later recalled the defen-

Fig. V. Colonel Joseph Bondy.

dant in his "first case" as "one of many of the young urchins of the seventh ward who made their way in life" (p. vii).¹

"Willie" was six years of age in 1883 when he, his sister Anna, younger brother Jack and mother arrived at *Castle Garden* in New York City before the immigrant facility at *Ellis Island* had been created for the reception of immigrants entering the United States. The family's breadwinner preceded their arrival two years earlier from Sweden where 'Willie' and his sister had been born. Meanwhile, he was saving for the rest of the family's passage which now included newborn Jack.

After the reunited family was settled in their Syracuse home, 'Willie' celebrated his *Bar Mitzvah* or confirmation in 1890. His father (*i.e.,* whose shortened last name became "Provol") soon thereafter became disabled after falling through the frozen crust of the *Erie Canal* in nearby Geddes under the weight of his loaded backpack. He had been delivering merchandise to salt-worker customers who were ice-bound in their quarters lining the adjacent shores. Henry then became a part-time cantor at the neighboring *Mulberry Street Synagogue* (*i.e.,* later to become *Congregation Adath Yeshurun*) where Rev. Jacob Levi was likewise serving as a part-time synagogue functionary after having left his previous capacities at *Temple Society of Concord* (Rudolph, *op. cit.,* pp. 72, 79–80, 100, 128, 162 & 198).

The jury trial was held in nearby Jamesville. Provol's (*op. cit.*) recapitulation of events misnamed the site as "Janesville" (pp. 67-80). A local newspaper's front page headlined the approaching trial as follows: "Willie Provol, the Syracuse Match Peddler, Arrested for Looting Jamesville Carpenter Shop" (*idem.,* p. 69). One observer at the trial "remarked that only the appearance, arm in arm, of a local priest and a Syracuse rabbi prevented a riot on the day of the trial" (Rudolph, *ibid.,* pp. 31–32 & 109).

Rev. Jacob Levi was the "Syracuse rabbi" in question. According to the 1855 City *census,* his occupation was listed as "teacher." Other sources of information have enumerated certain of his previous communal activities at *Temple Society of Concord,* as follows: "An early 'combination *hazzan-shochet-mohel,* synagogue functionary, reader, pastor, spiritual leader" *et al.* (Ginsburg, *op. cit.,* pp. 19–20). He was a landowner and citizen residing with his *mishpocha* on East Jefferson Street.

"Rabbi" Jacob Levy was a revered citizen and Hebrew School teacher—among other part-time pursuits—who tutored a class of *Bar Mitzvah* boys including Willie in his living room. Among those who had resided with Rev. Levy at the same address had been his nephew "Moses Rothschild, butcher." He died during the *Civil War* while assaulting Rebel fortifications in the *Battle of Lookout Mountain.* Rev. Levy had served as a Trustee of various Burial, Benevolent and Charitable Societies and had been elected as a four-term Alderman for the 7th Ward. He had often been mentioned in Democratic Party circles as a potential Mayoral candidate.

Beneath the *post*-acquittal newspaper headline (*i.e.,* captioned above) which Provol later recalled, the published account reputedly stated:

"Willie Provol, the seventh ward newsboy and match peddler, was found not guilty of the charge of robbery at Ja[n[sville, as it was proven by Joseph Bondy, the young Syracuse lawyer, the charge was a put-up job by Weatherstone, owner of the Ja[n[sville country store, to create prejudice against peddlers, in order to get the town officials to pass a prohibitory license law." (Provol, *op. cit.,* pp.79-80).

ERIE CANAL CIRCUS-BOAT PERFORMER AND *CAYUGA LAKE* STEAM-BOAT CONCESSIONAIRE

It was a common occurrence for street 'urchin' chums—re-quoting the earlier parlance of Colonel Bondy (1937, *op. cit.*)—to travel far and wide offering their 'sundry notions' for sale. Weather conditions, unpredictable train schedules and other extenuating circumstances found them without an ability to communicate their whereabouts to family members. Some stuck close to home delivering local telegraphs.

A few extended families had sufficient resources to establish a permanent place of business (*Fig. VI*). Other male off-spring often scattered themselves amidst the rural countryside—at great risk to themselves—to target perceived "would be" rural patrons. Prominent among local public heath issues—even in New York City (www.VirtualJewishLibrary.org)—-was the then still controversial practice among the general population of pasteurizing dairy milk for human consumption.

Youngsters, such as 'Willie'—while doubling as a one-man variety singer and dancer, talented juggler, minstrel or acrobat—could also be quite entertaining as an overnight guest of farm family hosts. In the Yiddish vernacular, he would have undoubtedly achieved a reputation as a *"tummler."* It is not surprising that 'Willie's' father, on more than one occasion, found it necessary, to file a "missing person" report with the police after an extended absence from Syracuse (Provol, *op. cit.,* p. 52). Leaving the hurly-burly of city life to satisfy a 'hankering for the outside world' must have continued to stir his inner thoughts.

Much of the text in the aforementioned *The Pack Peddler* is attributable to Willie's' so-called "autobiographical memory." Others have characterized such data as generally telescopic, dynamic and lacking in autonomy. An autobiographer's memory is ordinarily thought to be "in a constant state of flux, is constantly being reorganized, and is constantly being subject to changes which the[ir] present tend to impose" (Kris, 1956, p. 299).

Another Syracusan chum of 'Willie' was Sam [Sime] 'Shimkey' Ferguson[2] with whom we'll become more acquainted in a subsequent section. They

Fig. VI. Cohen's Big Canal Store [Artist Van Vliet's 1952 rendition of a photographed scene of unknown vintage archived at the *Onondaga Historical Association Museum and Research Center*]

grew up as next-door neighbors who practiced somersaults and acrobatic stunts in a nearby hayloft. In the further words of 'Willie' (1937):

> "Sig Sa[u]telle owned and operated a canal boat circus [*Fig. VII*], which traveled up and down the Erie and Oswego Canals, performing in all the small towns . . . 'Shimkey' and I applied for a position in his circus. After a tryout, he hired us at a salary of four dollars a week and board . . . Sa[u]telle's circus boat was an attraction as it floated up and down the Oswego and Erie canals. On each side of the boat were paintings of circus acts, clown and animals. As the boat floated down the canal it resembled one of Ringling Brothers and Barnum circus billboards. The boat contained very comfortable living quarters for the performers. It had a luxurious dining room that seated over one hundred people. Sig made his home on this boat for a number of years. . . . After the shows at night he entertained his many friends of years standing in the various towns in his quarters. Sig was loved by every performer . . . [and] advertised 'Shimkey' and me as the youngest acrobatic team in the United States. As ringmaster, before each performance, he made a very flattering speech, or 'ballyhoo,' about our performance, after which the band played a 'fanfare' and we made our entrance into the sawdust ring amid cheers and applause. As we proceeded with our stunts, we were a hit. Thundering applause brought us back for many encores. After the performance, Sig hurried back to our dressing tent, complimented us on our success, and raised our salary fifty cents a week" (pp. 34–35).

After Henry Provol learned about son 'Willie's' circus activities, he put an abrupt stop to them. Before 'Willie' finalized further sojourns away from home, a successor employer first became amenable to his following *proviso*:

> "The only request we made was that we be allowed to leave for home each Friday afternoon, explaining that we had to observe the Jewish Sabbath and also take care of the Sunday newspaper route. As Saturday and Sunday were his most quiet days, he readily agreed. The guests were usually at the Falls, yachting, or horse-back riding on week-ends" (p. 103).

The next scheme—as seen through Willie's eyes—began as a consequence of his 'barnstorming' in rented Town Halls "within a radius of fifty miles of Syracuse" presenting a free song and dance show with handbills circulated in advance touting "Thalheimer's Fancy Gilt Edge Bond Stationery." The variety presentation featured "our colored pickaninny . . . [outfitted in] . . . a red velvet suit, white vest and a small derby hat" with our mascot bull-dog "named Bond" wearing a red blanket with a sign advertising our Troupe (pp. 95–96). A decorated wagon transported the itinerant troubadours between engagements. We distributed a beautiful engraved vendor's brass inkwell as "an additional free souvenir with each twenty-five cent sale" (p. 93).

Fig. VII. Sig Sautelle's Circus Canal Boat: "The BELLE."

During the following summer:

"We continued toward Cayuga Lake. A lake steamer made round trips between Cayuga Junction and Ithaca . . . Leaving our wagon at the junction, we packed our bags and boarded the steamer. As the steamer started, Chalky brought out his mouth organ, while Wash did his song and dance act. Finnegan then sang a couple of Irish ballads, while 'Red' and I closed with our acrobatic act. We had several boxes of stationery ready as I started my usual sales talk. While we were accustomed to selling one box each to the farmers and small town folks, these people were buying two and three boxes for their needs, as most of the passengers were vacation bound for the various lake resorts. A strikingly pretty, well dressed young lady handed me a two dollar bill, accepting only one box of stationery in exchange. She complimented us on the excellence of our performance and presented each of us with an American Beauty Rose from the bouquet she carried . . . When the steamer docked at Aurora, our first stop, there was a great crowd waiting. A uniformed band was playing Yankee Doodle as welled into the landing, and a cheer went up from every throat. A reception committee of young ladies, dressed in white . . . followed by two men in Uncle Sam's uniforms, bearing a banner which read" 'Welcome First Lady of the Land" . . . The beautiful lady who had . . . presented each of us with one of her roses, was none other than the former Frances Folsom, then Mrs. Grover Cleveland, wife of the President of the United States, married a short time before, in the White House. She was returning, as the guest of honor, to [Wells] College, where she had formerly been a student. As the boat pulled away from the dock, we could see the beautiful and colorful procession winding up the hill to the campus. Thereafter, in all my sales talks, I mentioned the fact that even Mrs. Grover Cleveland, the President's wife, used Thalheimer's Gilt Edge Writing Paper! . . . [At the *Cayuga Lake Hotel* (*Fig. VIII*)[3]

Fig. VIII. Cayuga Lake Hotel [Etching by unknown artist portraying hotel and landing with the lake steamer *"The ISABEL"* at dock in Sheldrake, N. Y. (Courtesy of *The History Center in Tompkins County*)].

with no place to stay] I explained to the manager that we were only peddlers and performers, on our way to visit Watkins Glen . . . [and humbly said] If you will accommodate us, we will pay you in stationery and give your guests a free show . . . After hearing our story, he said, 'All right, take these boys over to the annex' . . . It rained all that evening, so the guests were all gathered in the lobby . . . I arranged with the manager to clear the center of the floor for our performance . . . [and he] agreed to our selling stationery to the guests, as it was not customary for the hotels to furnish stationery as they do today . . . After the show, I made my usual sales talk, and raised the price to fifty cents a box instead of the usual twenty-five. I felt that these people had more money to spend and were accustomed to paying more than the farmers and small town folks to whom we had been selling. I also had in mind the hotel bill which had to be paid in the morning. I was pleasantly surprised, however, when the guests did not protest at the price of fifty cents, and many gave us a dollar and told us to keep the change . . . The next morning I was called to the private office and was none too confident as I entered the august presence of the proprietor . . . ' You know, sir, we made a deal with you to pay our bill in stationery,' I said . . . Then smiling whimsically, he asked 'Why are you shavers away from home?' I told him of being the sole support of my family and the other boys were poor, trying to assist their parents financially . . . 'Young man, if there were more boys like you in the world, there would be less poverty and suffering in the homes. I, too, was a poor boy on the streets of London when I was your age' . . . 'Just a minute. How would you boys like to finish the season at my hotel . . . I will charge you nothing for your board and you can occupy the same rooms. All I will ask will be to entertain my guests in the evening. You may have the privilege of selling your stationery and keeping all of your tips.' I had told him in the course of our conversation about selling the stationery to Mrs. Grover Cleveland on the steamer. 'I am the owner of that steamer,' he added, 'and you may have the privilege of entertaining and selling your stationery on the steamer also' . . . (pp. 97–103).

OTHER ADOLESCENT ACTIVITIES

The reader is reminded that the *fin-de-siécle* decade of 'Willie's' life stretched from age 13 through age 20. He was one of seven children amidst a burgeoning immigrant populace. Interspersed within the autobiographer's "first person" text are a series of encapsulated excerpts abbreviated, in part, thusly:

" . . . I was an excellent Hebrew scholar [*Fig. IX*] as a result of the training I received from my grandfather. The other boys had never seen a Swedish Jew, so I was somewhat of a curiosity to them (p. 8) . . . Mother shed many a tear when I put the eighty cents in her hand as my contribution towards the family's finances. Of course she would have rather seen me in school, but I felt that inasmuch Dad had such a struggle to make ends meet, that I, the oldest son, should help . . . To attend

Fig. IX. Rev. Max Wechsler with his Hebrew class in 1899 [Earlier class than one taught by Rev. Jacob Levy that 'Willie' attended].

public school was out of the question for me—I was in the business world and there I was fated to stay (p. 26) ... The parlor match ... called the safety match, was a great improvement over the sulphur matches, although they were expensive and were only used by persons of wealth. They were imported from Sweden and carried a high duty ... the United States Congress in 1890 was to eliminate the duty on the parlor match ... I started out as a match peddler ... after the import duty had been removed ... [when an arresting] Irish cop ... hustled me off to the police station in the patrol wagon ... " (pp. 45–46).[4]

'Willie' was never known to have been convicted of any crime; yet, he delighted in glibly caricaturing Syracuse's Irish-American cops with whom he who had several "brushes" as a juvenile. His descriptions of hotly contested games at *Star Park* between the *Berenstein Baseball Club* and *Murphy's Shamrocks*—in which he participated as a young boy—are likewise colorful (pp. 16–17).

EARLY ADULTHOOD PURSUITS

When 'Willie' later had occasion to reminisce about his family's brief sojourn in Brooklyn, he wrote:

"I was sixteen and my brother Jack fourteen years of age. He assisted me in the morning until school time by selling newspapers on the street cars. He also did my bookkeeping, as I could neither read nor write ... My career as a newsboy ended in disaster ... [*i.e.,* conflagration obliterated rented premises of his thriving corner newstand] ... Mother and Father held a family conference. They decided I had been through enough vicissitudes and it was now time I learned a trade. Mother had a cousin, Sam Samuels, who was a foreman in a large cigar factory in Binghamton, New York.[5] While on a recent visit, he had suggested that we move ... [since there were] ... new factories being established [which] ... would make [Dad] a fertile field in which to pack peddle ... Soon we were located in a cottage ... in an Irish neighborhood. There was only one other Jewish family living there. Binghamton was then known as "The Parlor City of America," and was a booming town ... [and] ... looked promising to Dad. He bought a horse and wagon, and began to sell dry goods and clothing to the cigar makers on the installment plan, a dollar down and a dollar a week ... Each boy and girl at the age of thirteen or fourteen would get a job at the cigar factory, learning the trade, working from fourteen to sixteen hours every day. The workers were crowded into rooms without proper ventilation with gas jets as the only light. Between the tobacco smell and the leaky gas jets, I have often wondered how any of us left the factory alive ... (pp. 119–124).

The garment industry had long before dominated Rochester's commerce. In 1892, the *Rhine Street Shul* was formed by immigrants:

" . . . not wishing to worship in synagogues already established by the earlier immigrants [who] . . . built their own synagogue . . . [which] attracted a large number of tailors and in 1896 became known as the *Congregation of Tailors, or the Chevra Chayteem"* . . . " (Kasdin, 2005, p. 6).

Whether or not the gender-related activities of Jewish girls included family responsibilities as "mother's helper" and/or home-based "piece work," many undoubtedly also participated in the "needle trades" throughout upstate New York.

Part D

SYRACUSE'S 'DER RABBINER'

The Reverend Dr. Adolph Guttman (also known as Rabbi Adolph B. Guttman, D.D. and hereafter often referenced as '*Der Rabbiner*,' his German-Yiddish sobriquet) arrived in 1883 at the *Temple Society of Concord (Fig. X)*, a Reform Congregation in Syracuse. He came well recommended, directly from the town of Liepnik in Moravia. Liepnik was renowned as a center of Jewish studies, and Adolph Guttman belonged to one of the learned families of that town (Rudolph, *op. cit.,* p. 198).

As Rudolph put it:

> "At first [he] preached in German, and after he had learned to speak the English language, he refused to preach in it until he had acquired a proper pronunciation. In this he followed the advices given by Dr. Gustave Gottheil who said 'Practice before a mirror and pronounce the words with the "th." When you have mastered the pronunciation, the message to your congregation will be impressive, but it cannot be so when your pronunciation of English words raises a titter or laughter.' Not until he was fully satisfied that he had mastered speaking without an accent did Dr. Guttman preach in English" (*ibid.,* p. 198).[1]

Der Rabbiner, in 1887, married Marilla Goldstein, a native Syracusan and public school teacher from 1874 to 1884. She was among the participants in the drive that led to the creation of the *Jewish Orphan Asylum of Western New York* (Rudolph, 1970, p. 198). The congregation of *Temple Society of Concord* gave them a wedding present of $400.00 (*ibid.,* p. 199). She later became the Sunday school principal.

Fig. X. Board of Trustees of Temple Society of Concord [Seated from left to right, Benjamin Bronner, William Henochsberg & Adolph Guttman; standing from left to right, August Falker, Lee Schoener, Gates Thalheimer & David Danziger (Courtesy of *Temple Society of Concord*)].

In addition to *Der Rabbiner's* adjunct duties as a Syracuse University Professor of Semitic Languages (*ibid.,* p. 245), he served as a part-time chaplain at the State Penitentiary in Auburn (*i.e.,* a railroad destination approximately 25 miles westward from Syracuse) where the father of the Kier brothers was incarcerated.

M. PEISSACKWOTCH = 'THE PASSOVER-WATCHER' = *'HERR M'*

A survey of late 19th-century conditions prevalent in various youth-boarding institutions was apparently conducted by a German-writing educator-administrator while he was traveling in North America. Judging from the tenor of certain of the ensuing passages, he was endeavoring to educate 'Old World' colleagues about the 'New World' status of some of their former students.

The sojourning author—a probable *landsman* of *Der Rabbiner*—identified himself in his journalistic narratives as "M. Peissackwotch." Such a last name is roughly translatable as "The Passover-Watcher" from its Yiddishist "pen name" equivalent.[2] *'Herr M'* is the *nom de plume* hereafter invoked in distinguishing him *vis-à-vis* other figures.

THE KIER BROTHERS

According to a 2007 English translation of Peissackwotch's (n.d.) cited German text:

> " . . . [Rabbi Dr. Guttman] told me that 12–13 years ago, he got to know an imprisoned man serving a 3 year sentence for theft. Upon his release, he wished to [reunite] his family, consisting of a wife and 4 sons with him in America. With the assistance of some charity, she received the means to go to Koenigsberg with the children. [There] she found that her money was not enough to get to America with the 4 boys; so, she left the two eldest sons—boys of 12 and 13 years—with the Rabbi, at the time, Dr. Bamberger . . . " (pp. 746–747).

Assuming from the archived typescript that *Herr M* shifted tenses by deploying "us" and "we" as authorial pronouns, a reader would be warranted in interpreting the next paragraph of his translated text as follows:

> "He in turn sent us the two boys. The eldest, who was a bit retarded, expressed the desire upon reaching the age of 14 to become a cabinet maker whereupon we apprenticed him to a competent cabinet maker. At that time, the parents wrote .

.. that we should send the boys to them. In the interest of the two boys, we did not follow the desire expressed by the parents since we knew that if the boys got over there without learning a trade the parents would make them peddlers or assign them similar types of work. Once the older son completed his apprenticeship and the second had learned to be a gardener for approximately 2½ years, we sent the boys to Syracuse" (*ibid.*).

If we again endow *Herr M's* text with a "first person' framework of reference, his narrated account resumed thusly:

"Before my departure, I received still another letter from the two young people in which they informed me that they had saved $1,000.00 and desired to buy a farm in th vicinity of Syracuse for a price of approximately $4,000.00, which should be feasible in that region in terms of its size; the money they lacked would be then sent to them by the Jewish Agricultural and Industrial Aid Society at favorable terms. Later on I visited the boys in their house and found that they had a very nice apartment with 3 bedrooms as well as a dining room and parlor. They had built nearly all of the furniture themselves. This family, which previously had been a burden on the community since the father did little work, attained a certain level of comfort due to the efforts of two well raised boys, so that the entire family desired to live on the land as well, based on the description of the two boys of their life and they would later, one might surmise, become good farmers as well. I have discussed this case in such great detail in order to demonstrate that among the Russian Jews it is not the parents who raise the children to be craftsmen and farmers but rather the children who bring the parents to perform practical work" (pp. 750–751).

Implicit within the final sentence of the above-quoted passage by the otherwise anonymous author is his belittlement of the 'Old World' ways of the two youths' parents. According to his prognoses, it was futile to countenance the likelihood that Russian parents emigrating to the United States (*i.e.,* an environment plagued by rampant urban poverty) might nevertheless—as Levy (*op. cit.*) condescendingly put it—"wean them from the tendency to 'dealing' and 'peddling,' which is almost hereditary with them" (p. 13). The 'transformative' undertone voiced by *Herr M* favored the 'steering' of young men into productive work as craftsmen or farmers—even at the risk of familial estrangements—as an alternative to what was perceived as their 'drifting' into stereotyped "Jewish" pursuits.

Part E

YOUNG MEN'S HEBREW ASSOCIATIONS

A June 8, 1888 column in the *Tidings* reported that the Jewish citizens of Syracuse "contributed $2,000.00 toward the YMCA building" (p. 2). Five years afterwards, the '*Panic of 1893*' was said to have "killed the national . . . YMHA of America" (*Fig. XI*) movement (Adler & Connolly, 1960, p. 243). Perhaps the lack of sufficient space for indoor athletic activities coupled with an over-abundance of outdoor seasonal space became significant concurrent factors. In Syracuse, temporary quarters had been situated in *Rubin's Hall* until room at the *Zenner Block* was rented. Ultimately, the *Marshall Homestead* was made available coupled with the construction of an adjoining facility.[1] From the vantage point of a pair of Buffalo historians (*ibid.*):

> "When the 'Y' movement caught new breath with business recovery, it interested itself in the Americanization of immigrants . . . The new "Y" of this period often served as a place of refuge for foot-loose adolescents, for its clubhouse offered cultural outlets not to be found in the downtown synagogues and other immigrant organizations . . . [In Buffalo] . . . we know . . . [that they] met in a Walnut Street house in the 1890s. . . . [and] placed increasing emphasis on the popular cult of self-improvement. Its members sponsored a Literary Club, promoted oratorical contests, arranged musical evenings, presented dramatic productions and engaged in athletic contests" (*ibid.*)

By 1895 in Buffalo (*ibid.*), the activities of a counterpart organization of "young men and women . . . .were almost exclusively bowling and whist" (p. 204).[2]

Fig. XI. Y.M.H.A. (left); *Marshall Home* (right).

JEWISH CHAUTAUQUA SOCIETY

The *Jewish Chautauqua Society* was founded in 1893. It also was patterned after an earlier Christian-oriented "summer assembly" which annually met at an enclave along the shores of *Lake Chautauqua* south of Buffalo. The "satellite" Jewish off-spring, incorporated under the laws of the neighboring state of Pennsylvania, initially negotiated an agreement with the *Chautauqua Literary and Scientific Circle*. A system of popular education known as the "Chautauqua System" was thereupon nationally promoted by Rabbi Henry Berkowitz of Philadelphia (*Fig. XII*). Arrangements were made for Dr. Lee K. Frankel (*i.e.,* who later became manager of the *United Hebrew Charities*) to participate in the parental organization's summer assemblies, pedagogical programs and seminars (Lowenstein, 1932, p. 121). Together with "Chancellor" Berkowitz, he assisted in the formulation of a series of *syllabi* for publication by the *Jewish Chautauqua Society*. Jewish students in upstate New York and elsewhere thereby became privy to an intellectual brand of "home/group" learning which they otherwise might not have been able to access.

THE JEWISH CHAUTAUQUA SOCIETY.

P. O. BOX 825, PHILADELPHIA, PA.

This is a society for popular education in Jewish History and Literature. It is based on the famous Chautauqua System of Education. It has members enrolled from all parts of the Union, Canada and British India. You may enroll as an Individual Reader, a Home Circle Reader, or a Local Circle Reader, in any of the following courses:

GENERAL BIBLE COURSE.

A four years' course for the general reader and devoted to the literary and historical study of the Bible. Open to persons of all denominations and beliefs. You may begin at any time. A Syllabus, "The Open Bible," by Dr. H. Berkowitz, is provided, outlining each year's reading, and giving full directions. The completion of the four years' course secures a certificate.

Enrollment fee, 50 cents for each year.

Fig. XII. A Publication of the Jewish Chautauqua Society [addendum to text of *Kiddush or Sabbath Sentiment in Home* by Dr. Henry Berkowitz (1898)].

Der Rabbiner, as reported in the *Tidings* on October 27, 1893, continued with his series of lectures on the "The Elements of Civilized Life." He spoke last Friday evening on "Education," and made a strong appeal in behalf of the *Chautauqua Literary and Scientific Circle*:

"There is no time limit on one's self-improvement. Only the young high school graduates of sixteen or seventeen imagine that they have finished their education; only the young men, wasting the golden hours at the card table and in gambling, think that they know it all and need learn no more. But those who know something feel that they cannot afford to fritter away their golden hours and precious opportunities in shallowness and emptiness. Education is as easy to be had today as the air we breathe or water we drink. It does not require any extraordinary ability; all that it requires is a noble ambition. Old and young, men and women, rich and poor, all ought to avail themselves of the splendid opportunities that is offered by the *Chautauqua Circle*" (p. 7).

He was also traveling to Ithaca once a month on Sundays to lead what today might be termed as an "outreach program" of Jewish education.

In a more current context, Ross Frederick (2008) reported that the *Chautauqua Institution's* grounds will soon house a 7,600 square foot $2,000,000.00 structure (*i.e.,* known as the *Everett Jewish Life Center*). It will anchor one phase of the *Abrahamic Program* to which the *Chautauqua Institution* is now committed. According to the current Director: "The addition of a "Jewish Life Center"—and eventually a Muslim one—will advance that goal . . . " (p. 1). The newspaper article states that both the *Hebrew Congregation of Chautauqua* and the *Chabad of Chautauqua* "will [then each] have a home of their own: a two story [edifice] with a wide porch, a kosher kitchen, a library and five apartments" (*ibid.*) where visitors can gather for lectures, discussions, movies and socializing.

There admittedly was an exclusionary practice in the 1950's when Jews were not welcome to buy property; more recently, summer daily lectures and concerts have attracted audiences that are estimated to be 25% Jewish. How the Jewish-Center fares under the local entity's "non-denominational" framework coupled with the parental organization's oversight might provide a microcosm for study by future generations of social scientists. Coincidentally, an analogous "end-of-a-*millennium's*-look-forward-projection" was in fact voiced just before mid-night on December 31, 1899 (*Appendix 1*).

COLLEGE-BASED ORGANIZATIONS

By the reckoning of Syracuse's correspondent on March 14, 1890, "the *Tidings* thinks there is something suggestive in the fact that we have four college students while Rochester has only one" (p. 3). The importance of education had earlier been stressed in a sermon by Rev. Dr. [Joseph] Stolz (1888) delivered at *Zion Temple* in Chicago:

"Since [he] is a native of Syracuse [*i.e.,* also first cousin of Louis Marshall]—so near your city—I thought that your readers would be interested in an abstract . . . He also alluded to the meagre attendance of our youth in the high schools of this city . . . and deplored the singular apathy of parents in allowing their sons to idle away their time in mercantile purposes for which most of the young men of today have a great predilection because it gives them more spending money and a greater number of pernicious amusements which are fast undermining their physical as well as mental condition. He was outspoken when he advised his hearers not to listen to the boys when they cajoled and begged to be allowed to go into 'business' ... their sons ... swagger through life somehow, but they remain ignoramuses for the rest of their lives ... " (p. 7).

For a feminist perspective, *Der Rabbiner's* sermons delivered a pair of sermons on successive Friday evenings in Syracuse during February of 1891 were entitled "A Young Woman's Possibilities" and "Woman's Rights" respectively. Their full message has been further extracted from the text quoted in the *Tidings* April 3, 1891 issue (*op. cit.*), to wit:

"Woman, you have the right to live independently of any social laws and regulations which are injurious to health, which prevent the culture of heart and mind, and which are detrimental to your development into a true, sincere and worthy woman. Woman, you have a right to lead a useful, active life. Happy the woman who lives in the full enjoyment of some useful activity. In this country, where we are subjected constantly to commercial reverses, there is no man, I care not what his wealth or position may be, who is absolutely sure that his daughter, or his wife even, may not some day be compelled to earn her own living. Let every young woman learn to do some kind of work by which she may be able, if thrown upon her own resources, to take care of herself, independent of father, brother or husband" (p. 7).

A drastic "falling off" in the participation of college-aged youths in Jewish-related activities occurred during the "Gay Nineties." So-called "Greek" fraternities and sororities were not ordinarily open to Jewish students *per se*. Even upon a friendly 'blended' basis, certain strains of Orthodox Jewry were often an anathema to prospective "brothers" or "sisters." Until the advent of a national network of *campus*-based "Hillel" settings in 1923, few venues existed where these maturing undergraduates felt welcomed in such an intellectually cross-fertilized environment.

U.S.S. OLYMPIA

Presumably "any boy who says he is between 15 and 17 years of age, over 5 feet in height and over 100 pounds in weight" (*i.e.,* according to governing Regulations shortly before the *Spanish-American War*) could apply for enlistment as a 'seaman apprentice' at a United States Naval Yard. One such applicant was none other than Samuel (*a/k/a* Sime or 'Shimkey') Ferguson. To re-quote the earlier parlance of Colonel Bondy (1937, *op. cit.*), he may be recalled as 'Willie's' Syracuse "urchin" pal and former acrobatic partner with *Sig Sautelle's Canal Boat Circus* "at a salary of four dollars a week and board" (Provol, *op. cit.,* p. 34). Samuel was billeted as the "apprentice signal boy" aboard the *U.S.S. Olympia,* Commodore George Dewey's flagship, at the *Battle of Manila Bay* (*Fig. XIII*).

Fig. XIII. Apprentice signal boy Samuel Ferguson (top far left) [Others standing with Commodore George Dewey, second from right on bridge of *U.S.S. Olympia* at the *Battle of Manila Bay* on May 1, 1898 were Marine orderly John H. McDougall & Chief Yeoman Merrick W. Creagh at far right (Courtesy of *Naval Historical Center*)].

The adult 'Willie' extolled the heroics of his juvenile cohort in his retrospective, albeit "hearsay," account of the events:

" . . . As every schoolboy knows, Admiral Dewey steamed into Manila Bay and destroyed the entire Spanish fleet without the loss of man or vessel. After this murderous bombardment, a white flag was hoisted over Fort Cavite, and Sime Ferguson was in charge of the boat which Admiral Dewey ordered lowered to take down the Spanish flag and hoist in its place the Stars and Stripes. As Ferguson's small boat pulled toward the fort, the Spaniards opened fire on it; however, their fire was returned by a heavy bombardment from the American ships. Ferguson was caught in the storm of shells and explosives. He did not turn back however. This intrepid Jewish Yankee completed his mission. He hauled down the Spanish flag, and sent up to the top of the staff 'Old Glory' . . . " (p. 37)

Returning to the war-time activities of Theodore Roosevelt, he led his "Rough Riders" into battle against Cuba. After they quickly vanquished the enemy, he embarked upon a *jingoistic* campaign in October of 1898 for election as New York State's Governor.[3] The *Spanish Inquisition* had left deep scars upon Jewish consciousness. In the Philippine uprising which began on May 1, 1898:

" . . . Buffalo Jews answered the call to duty. It has been observed, and probably correctly, that throughout the country Jews wished to see Spain humbled, for they had never forgotten the 1492 expulsion at the hands of Ferdinand and Isabella" (Adler & Connolly, *op. cit.,* p. 219).

A political handbill circulated by a Rochester Jewish-Republican organization urged Jews to vote for Colonel Roosevelt as the 1898 gubernatorial candidate on the grounds that he "had helped humble *anti-*Semitic Spain in the recent *Spanish-American War*" (*ibid.*, p. 474). In New York City:

"The Lower East Side was flooded with handbills, printed in Yiddish, signed by 'Jewish members of the Republican State Committee.' The flyers urged Jewish voters tom cast their ballots for gubernatorial candidate Theodore Roosevelt, who the year before had led his Rough Riders in their famous charge up San Juan Hill in Santiago, Cuba. The Rough Riders' victory, combined with other triumphs at sea and on land during the Spanish-American War, led Spain to surrender her colonies in Cuba and the Philippines. The Yiddish flyers addressed to Jewish voters bore the title, 'WHO TAKES REVENGE FOR US?' Its opening sentence made the answer clear: 'Every respectable citizen, every good American and every true Jew, must and will vote for the Republican gubernatorial candidate—*Theodore Roosevelt*" (www.JewishVirtualLibrary.org).

RIPENING OF ECUMENICAL DIALOGUE

Der Rabbiner annually shared his pulpit with the pastor of the neighboring *May Memorial Unitarian Church* which had been founded by Rev. Samuel J. May, the famous abolitionist cleric. Soon Dr. Guttman ingratiated himself with the local gentile world as an interfaith humanitarian with a social conscience. Nevertheless, reverberations from the Jewish diaspora beyond the *Statue of Liberty* continued to percolate throughout North America. The *Dreyfus Affair* in France and pogroms in Russia coupled with the initial *Zionist Conference* in Switzerland were beginning to fuel the approaching 20th-century's conscience.

Part F

THE *FRESH AIR FUND*

Some time in 1895-1896, *Der Rabbiner* and *Herr M* alongside him departed from Syracuse—undoubtedly *via* scheduled railway service—to the village of Freeville. It was there, approximately 50 miles in a southerly direction, that the recently founded *George Junior Republic* (hereafter referenced as the "*Republic*") was situated (*Fig. XIV*). One might reasonably assume that their interest was influenced, in part, by the fact that a significant number of the *Republic's* first citizens had been brought up in New York City with a readily identifiable Jewish background. Archival records and contemporary diary entries amply support the latter premise.[1]

The *credo* of the resulting miniature community in Freeville had been generally modeled after contemporary standards of the larger adult society and

Fig. XIV. Hotel, assembly hall, court house and jail, residence of Mr. George [p. 285].

envisioned a self-governing entity run by its citizen-members. Few minors or juveniles in the State of New York, without a sponsoring parent or foster patron—whether related or unrelated—had access to such *non*-sectarian istitutions during the *fin-de-siécle* decade of the 19th-century. *Der Rabbiner* and *Herr M* continued with their focus upon ghetto-born lads and girls whose basic heritage still seemed Jewish-oriented although it was gradually blending into the greater pluralistic society.

Although the *Republic* was not formally organized until 1895 (*Fig. XV*), the underlying concept was begun by William R. George (*i.e.*, 'Daddy' as he quickly became affectionately known) in New York City during the summer of 1890 as an "off-shoot" of the *New York Tribune's* so-called "Fresh Air Fund." It evolved from an annual summer sojourn for urbanized youth into a long-term haven—five years later—for youths (*i.e.*, without an active caretaking parent [*Figs. XVI & XVII*]) in upstate New York. 'Daddy,' was the institution's first leaders. He

" . . . .had been born on a farm in West Dryden and at the age of fourteen removed with his family to New York City. Rebelling against the set regime of preparatory school and college, he had turned his energies directly to things

Fig. XV. The original "Residents"—Winter of 1895-96 ("Daddy" top right) [p. 293].

Fig. XVI. A minor—10 YEARS OF AGE [p. 448].

Fig. XVII. Charley and his guardian [p. 439]

that interested him, chiefly social work among small boys in the slums...he began what was to develop into the most interesting social experiment of the times . . . he took about fifty boys and girls into the country, housing them in a building which a friend had turned over to him. This was at Freeville, a region where George had spent his boyhood . . . " (Chamberlain, 1935, pp. 222–223).

A MODEL *NON*-SECTARIAN ENTITY

Modern readers with more than a dozen decades behind us undoubtedly wonder how so-called 'social scientists' and—more importantly—the adolescents themselves may have perceived their future 'lots in life' at the *Republic* (*Figs. XVIII, XIX & XX*). Concomitantly, a Calvinistic-like fear of excessive leisure seemed to pervade 'Daddy's' philosophy of life in forging the *Republic's* future motto, to wit: *Nothing Without Labor!* (*Figs. XXI & XXII*).

Rather than reiterating the "Passover-Watching" traveler's translated text (Peissackwotch, *op. cit.*, pp. 750–751), the insights of certain sociologists

Fig. XVIII. "Aristocrats" [p. 287].

Fig. XIX. Officers of the battalion [p. 442].

Fig. XX. Baseball nine ("Daddy" top) [p. 445].

Fig. XXI. The laundry [p. 295].

Fig. XXII. Sewing class.

about the period in question have proven prescient. One such view was voiced by Matthew A. Crenson (*op. cit.*):

> "In the general movement to escape the artificial discipline of the asylum, some institutions turned earnestly anti-institutional. In the 1890's, a few experimenters established self-governing communities of children where the young citizens drew up their own constitutions, passed their own laws, and tried violators in their own courts. Some even issued their own currency, which inmates earned by labor and spent for meals, clothing, and lodging. The instated premise, apparently, was that institutional discipline became less limiting when the inmates imposed it upon one another. The best known of these juvenile democracies was the George Junior Republic at Freeville, New York, founded by William R. "Daddy" George in 1895. Theodore Roosevelt was one of the most enthusiastic admirers. Imitations of the George Junior Republic soon appeared in half a dozen states . . . " (pp. 115–116):

In 1897, the *American Journal of Sociology* published a two-part essay entitled "The Junior Republic" written by *Syracuse University* Prof. John R. Commons.[2] It was widely circulated and referenced both here and abroad. At the time, Mr. George had already served as the *Republic's* "General Superintendent." In Commons's reverential tribute about him, he wrote about the gradual metamorphosis in his subject's outlook:

" . . . His only purpose at the time was to give the boys and girls a thoroughly happy outing. The second summer—1891—he took a company of 200, all to be kept on one farm in tents, and from that time to the present the number has ranged from 150 to 200, of whom about one-fourth have been girls. The people and churches of the neighborhood responded bountifully with food and clothing, and these were distributed freely among the youthful claimants. Four summers of this experience children came for the food and the clothing that they could take back to their parents . . . Here were two conditions for Mr. George to meet, crime and pauperism, the very life and moving spirit of the political and charitable system of New York City and its tenements. And the fact that 200 of these budding criminals and paupers were on his hands made him think . . . . The next summer—1894—Mr. George determined to make them work for what they took home. Boxes of clothing sent in by the philanthropic were no longer passed around, but notice was given that only hard work with pick and shovel would be considered a claim for such. The grumbling and muttering were general and ominous. One boy, however, after a period of thinking, offered to work five days for a suit of clothes—the price set by Mr. George. The others hectored him and called him a fool for working to get what was his right, but when he walked away with his new suit, the pride of honest ownership, and the immediate capitulation of many others, were the first suggestion toward the Republic's cure for pauperism" (pp. 281–296).

The sense of private property remained a coveted value in the primarily agricultural colony 'Daddy' had been instrumental in originating. He not only targeted the so-called "pauperism" witnessed in New York City's slums amidst overcrowded tenements; but, also addressed the companion issue of crime in like manner" (*op. cit.*):

" . . . [He] made rules against smoking, gambling, stealing, fighting, etc., but how to punish for violations were beyond his comprehension. He even tried the whip . . . Finally, in 1894, he inaugurated a public trial of every alleged offender, the decision to be awarded by the town meeting. On the suggestion of the boys a jury of the best citizens was selected by Mr. George himself for such trials. At this time instead of corporal punishment he substituted fines of a graded number of hours' work" (pp. 282–284).

During this era, 'Daddy' formulated the underlying principles which would serve as the *Republic's* guideposts. The first four governing rules he initially promulgated were:

"1. The citizens of the *Republic* may carry out the idea of the Social Sanitarium as a treatment idea, instead of the punishment method embodied in the state prison system;
2. The citizens of the *Republic* shall be of both sexes. Under no circumstances may this rule be changed;

3. No boy or girl shall be debarred from citizenship because of his race or religion;

4. No person shall be debarred from the Board of trustees because of his race or religion."

The citizens' religious affiliations were varied. Arrangements for their 'off-*campus*' religious services were facilitated at Auburn and other sites likewise accessible from the nearby Freeville railway station. Protestant and Roman Catholic religious services were readily available although none of the *Republic's* citizens had any obligation to attend either or any of them unless subject to the fulfillment of a judicially imposed mandate.[3]

A REPENTANT SON?

Appendix 2 replicates a document found in the *"William R. George Family Papers, 1750-1989,"* written—according to its Correspondence Register—on October 9, 1899. One is able to ascertain that the letter-writer had served as the *Republic's* Police Chief (*Fig. XXIII*). A German sociologist (Munster-

Fig. XXIII. Chief of police [p. 441].

berg, 1902), writing about the *Republic's* punishment criteria)—and more particularly offenses committed in 1896 and 1897—noted:

> "The office of policeman is about the most respectable and desirable in the republic. To attain it an examination is required. The policemen are paid out of the taxes and are dressed in uniform. Each is responsible to the police board, and like every officer, loses his position at once if he does not fill it conscientiously. He is severely punished for overlooking an offense or permitting a prisoner to escape; the misuse of his power brings a penalty . . . " (p. 672)

Absolute criteria of proper and improper conduct, governed by a "New England" town meeting philosophy of moral right and wrong, evolved in the lives of the *Republic's* adolescent and young adult citizens. Outsiders, like Commons, however seemingly exhibited a tendency to characterize the inhabitants in stereotyped terms (*Figs. XXIV & XXV*).

Fig. XXIV. A pauper [p. 288].

Fig. XXV. "Neverworks" (p. 291).

THE *REPUBLIC'S* 'COLOR-BLIND' CHARACTER

Although the *Republic* made no discernable practice—during the era under examination—of categorizing its citizens upon a racial basis, archival correspondence discloses an instance in which "Daddy's" wife penned a *post*-script to a lengthy letter she wrote on October 4, 1897 as follows: "A colored boy [*i.e.,* 15 years of age is] coming tonight whose name I do not know." Other correspondence also discloses that American Indian children were likewise accommodated on an 'open door' basis.

Part G

EPILOGUE

How, you may ask, was the *Monograph* you have in hand conceived? Simply put, the archival 'springboard'—leading back to my native upstate New York—began in Manhattan. The early lives examined span a decade approximately 125 years ago.

Peer over my shoulder as I cross the threshold of an unpretentious side-entrance to a mansion fronting upon Fifth Avenue whose plaque announces: *YIVO Institute for Jewish Research*. A dignified elderly woman with an unmistakable Yiddish accent approaches me as I survey what must have once served as a grand drawing room. Every cubicle of enclosed space is bulging with oversized volumes. Is it the aroma of yellowing pages or the leathery scent of their ornate bindings that suffused the air?

"How may I help you," queries my amiable greeter?

After a measured pause, I express an interest in the history and culture of *Ashkenazi* Jewry in America. "Do you have a place in mind," she asks? I immediately mutter—Syracuse!—my birthplace. My library accomplice questions whether I have a preference for Yiddish, Russian, German or Hebrew printed texts. With little hesitation, I—in turn—respond: *"Deutsch!"*

I have actually begun thinking to myself about the stifling thrust of compound-worded nouns appearing in German newspapers. Several decades beforehand during my service in the *U. S. Army*, I had succeeded in deciphering the daily news in the *Frankfurter Allgemeine Zeitung*.

Without detouring to a catalog, my newfound guide ushers me to *YIVO's* "United States Territorial Collection" (*i.e.,* Archive #RG 117, Container 111) and examines the typescript of a text until we arrive at a passage captioned

"SYRAKUS." Then she takes it upon herself to furnish me with a German-English dictionary.

Admittedly, I was not oblivious to the fact that my parents had both studied in *Vilna* during their courtship. Yet, no other conscious link to the Archive in which I had ensconced myself was then known to me. I subsequently learned that my paternal grandparents came from *Svencionys* in what is now Lithuania while my maternal grandparents came from more distant *Vilkaviskas* and *Proskurov*.

Later at a family wedding in Brooklyn, a *Litvak* Rabbi asked me from where I came. Not fathoming that his inquiry might call for the identity of an ancestral *shtetl* in Lithuania, I innocently mentioned "Syracuse" and questioned if he knew where it was located. "Yes," he knowingly seemed to utter: "It is a tiny round dot on the map!"

Harold Bloom (2008) authored an essay in which he translated the same phrase (*i.e.*, "tiny round dot") from a Yiddish poem by Jacob Glatshteyn (*i.e.*, "1919") about his "comic vision of the poet lost in the streets of New York, yet better off than in an Eastern Europe awash with pogroms" (pp. 24–26). The exile, the *galut* is being compared—in poetic terms—to being lost in the darkness or a sense that other people are still continuing in their old ways in terms of spiritual longing.

Bloom explicated the poetic phrase thusly:

> " . . . *kleynshik pintele*, 'tiny round dot," refers to the proverbial Yiddish phrase dos pintele yid, the essence of Jewishness, and it puns on the dot of the letter *yud*, pronounced *yid*, which is the tiny vowel sign on the tiniest Hebrew letter. Desperately ironic and wildly gleeful, the brief lyric testifies to a mere but sufficient survival" (*ibid.*).

In spite of the slighting metaphorical rejoinder voiced by the aforementioned Brooklyn Rabbi, a family plot at Syracuse's *Frumah Packard Cemetery* is the "tiny round dot" upon a map of upstate New York where *Malchamovitz* may some day momentarily hover over my buried remains.

Notes

PART A

1. The mountain, lying on the border between East and West which was known as the Biblical Ark's final resting place in the wake of the devastation wrought by the divine-ordained flood. According to S. Joshua Kohn (1959): "At least one identifiable Utican, Erasmus H. Simon, was interested and so favorably impressed with Noah's visionary experiment that he not only commended Noah but offered his services. This we learn from Noah's letter of reply which has recently come to light and in which he decries the prejudice and suspicion which others have cast upon him. He emphasizes that his motives are genuine and that his hopes are high for the future success" (p. 7). The entire text of Noah's October 22, 1825 coupled with the above-cited author's footnotes is indispensable to an understanding of the correspondents' perception that the nearby Iroquois " . . . aborigines of America, are the descendants of our lost tribes . . . " (*ibid.*, pp. 7–9).

PART B

1. The *Rochester Jewish Children's Home* is the subject of a different study. Goldstein (1996) cited another authority who "recalls the 'new spirit' that marked the beginning of the new century, the era in which the *Rochester Jewish Children's Home* welcomes its first wards" (p. 36).

2. As one of his biographers remarked: "Mixed with this Americanism was a good portion of hometown loyalty; in later years, he sometimes acted as though no one from Syracuse could do any wrong" (Rosenstock, 1965, p. 28). Among his boyhood experiences, he (1929) recalled having " . . . salted hides and calfskins . . . [and] . . . never went to college for a single day . . . " (Reznikoff, pp. 1145–1147). Another biographer (Wise) stated that as a "country boy . . . [he] . . . has never completely

outgrown that background, has never, despite his many years of urban residence, become wholly citified . . . [yet] . . . played so many roles upon the Jewish scene that one might write about him at equal length as statesman, educator, religious revivalist, philanthropist . . . " (pp. 181–182). Melvil Dewey (1851–1931) of the New York State *Board of Regents* and the *Lake Placid Club* had used the official stationery of his department to distribute circulars of the *Lake Placid Club* in which Jews were characterized as "members of an undesirable and obnoxious group" (p. 187). Marshall, to whose attention the matter came, not only protested to the Governor about the action of Mr. Dewey, but demanded his removal from office upon the ground of discriminatory prejudice against a large element of the citizenry of the state of New York. So effective and vigorous was his action that it compelled Mr. Dewey's resignation" (p. 188). In a peripheral context, it is noted that other members of the Marshall family were, like him, enthralled by upstate New York's *Adirondack Preserve* throughout their lives. One son, after whom Montana's *Robert Marshall Wilderness Area* was named, obtained a *Ph.D.* degree in Forestry. His co-conservationist brother James also achieved recognition as an early environmental lawyer. In the waning years of the 19th-century, their father had acquired an interest in "Knollwood," the *Lower Saranac Lake* retreat where the family's summer home was situated. Albert Einstein and his wife, among others were welcomed as guest in a cabin at "Knollwood." It was there that news reached him about the detonation of an atomic bomb to end World War II. Einstein had met the elder Marshall in 1929 at an assembly of World Jewry in Zurich called to form an enlarged *Jewish Agency* in conjunction with the British mandate for Palestine. Louis Marshall not only participated in three of New York State's earlier *Constitutional Conventions* which led to the "Forever Wild" creation of the *Adirondack Preserve*; but, he was likewise instrumental in helping to found the *New York State College of Forestry* at *Syracuse University*.

3. Footnote 47 of Korn's treatise states as follows; "The name *YIVO*, which is more familiar to American Jews, is an abbreviation for *Yiddisher Vissenshaftlikher Institut*" (p. 22). As the preceding text noted: "The great *Jewish Encyclopedia of 1901-1905* . . . whose first appearances in America were in translation from German---and under the twin influences of the Vilna Yiddish Scientific Institute (the name is no accident) and the development of new concepts of social history in the United States" (pp. 9–10). "Of the original ten Jewish scholars who formed the editorial board, only Cyrus Adler was American trained," according to Korn. The preponderance of the work was originally composed in the German language during the *fin-de-siécle* decade.

PART C

1. In *Webster's Seventh New Collegiate Dictionary* (1969), an alternate definition for the word "urchin" is "a pert or roguish youngster" (p. 977).

2. A weekly columnist in *The Forward* writing, under the by-line "*Philologos,*" twice commented about the origins of the last name "Ferguson" (www.Forward.com): " . . . The well known joke I told in the same column about the Jewish immigrant 'Sean Ferguson' would seem to have a kernal of historical truth. *Forward*

reader Eldad Ganin has sent me the following excerpt from a geneological Web site called Avoteynu (Hebrew for 'Our Forefathers'). Posted by a researcher named Gary Mokotoff. Mr. Mokotoff writes in the excerpt, 'There really was a Sean Ferguson . . . . almost,' and tells us that the origins of the story have been traced to the case of one 'Samuel Forgotson,' who immigrated to the United States in the 1860s. According to his grandson, Tracy Ferguson of Syracuse, N. Y., Mr. Forgotson settled in upper New York State, where he Americanized his name to Ferguson. Tracy himself eventually became a fundraiser for a Jewish organization. And, Mr. Molotoff tells us: 'Tracy's associates pointed out that his peculiarly non-Jewish name, might be a detriment to his fund-raising ability, so Tracy turned disadvantage to advantage by inventing a story. He told his audience that his unusual name was derived in an unusual way when his grandfather, Samuel Forgotson, arrived at Ellis Island and blurted out in a moment of panic *"Shayn farges'n"* to the question 'What is your name?' The story brought gales of laughter from his audience, so Tracy continued to use it as a warm-up introduction to his appeal for funds . . . The story so caught the fancy of the public that it was passed from person to person until it became part of Jewish-American folklore.' Although as [another reader points out], Ellis Island was not yet an important immigrant station in the 1860s, this would indeed seem to be the source of the 'Sean Ferguson' story—and the story itself, it strikes me, may even have more truth in it than Mr. Mokotoff allows . . . Under the name of Samuel Forgotson, Sean Ferguson may have really existed' . . . "

3. 'Willie' was approximately four years of age when President Cleveland—born in Buffalo and having resided during part of his boyhood in Fayetteville—married Frances Folsom in 1886. It is more likely that the episode in question took place almost a decade later during his second term. Contrary to that part of his narrative stating that the lake-steamer in question was headed for "Watkins Glen Falls" at the foot of *Seneca Lake*, it would not have then been accessible *via* a ferry route from *Cayuga Lake*. Although 'Willie' probably made the over-land side-trip to "Watkins Glen Falls," the much nearer "Taughannock Falls" were likely to have been more frequented by hotel guests. One John E. Allen, who served as manager of the *Cayuga Lake Hotel*, was in all likelihood the individual who authorized 'Willie' to sell Thalheimer's gilt-edged stationery at both the *Cayuga Lake Hotel* and aboard it's lake steamer *"The Isabel."* Simultaneously, he also served as manager of the *Osborne House* in near-by Auburn hereinafter referenced in endnote 17.

4. Provol (*ibid.*) likewise stated that "The parlor matches had no sulphur odor and would light instantly while it required some time for the sulphur matches to ignite . . . Syracuse was soon overrun with match peddlers . . . The [local] salt workers had reasons for not wanting to change from the sulphur matches, as the salt sheds were infested with rats and the workers had great trouble in keeping them out of their homes. The brimstone matches served as a sort of rat trap, for soon as a rat smelled the sulphur, or swallowed the brimstone, it meant sure death" (pp. 43–48).

5. By way of contrast, Buffalo historians (Adler & Connolly, 1960) have noted that "cigar making seems to have been especially attractive to Jews . . . [It] was a popular immigrant business because a man could enter it with almost no capital and very little equipment. All he needed was a small room, a board, a knife and a supply of tobacco

leaves. After making his stock, he could then simply go out and peddle it" (p. 108). A cursory sampling of records for both the 1890 Federal *census* and the 1895 New York State *census* conducted for the cities of Buffalo, Rochester and Syracuse evidence numerous individuals listing their occupation as "cigar maker."

PART D

1. Significantly, "The *Rochester Jewish Tidings* reported the sermons of Dr. Guttman almost weekly in the Syracuse section of the newspaper, which gave the flavor of his personality and scholarship" (Rudolph, *op.cit.,* p. 296, fn. 9). Abraham J. Karp (1998), in a Chapter subtitled "From Campus to Pulpit: Simon Tuska of Rochester," illustrates how his subject, a pioneer in the American Rabbinate, was skeptical about the prospect of overcoming the 'language barrier' extant in the mid-19th-century. According to Karp: "Most congregations at the time conducted their services in Hebrew, with German as the language for congregational readings, preaching, and instruction" (*ibid.*). "If I am ever to accomplish some good by sermons," Tuska wrote," they must be delivered by me in English; and there are few congregations in this land, who can fully appreciate an *English* discourse. This will not cease to be the case until the rising American-born generation will have come to manhood. Then, no doubt, a fair field of labor will be spread before the *English* preacher . . . " (*ibid.*).

2. The implicit double entendre unveils a complex array of literary dilemmas.

PART E

1. Initially, the constitution of the local *Y.M.H.A.* stated that all Jewish young men over the age of 18 were eligible for membership. After the *Marshall Homestead* at 222 Cedar Street in Syracuse was donated (Handlin, 1957, p. xiii), an edifice was constructed upon an adjoining lot to house an expanded side-by-side institution.

2. Parlor four-handed card game pitting one twosome against another.

3. During "Teddy's" terms as New York City's elected Police Commissioner, he had appointed Jews to the force as well as a woman to hold an executive position. He conspicuously accepted an invitation to attend a protest parade against a "Sunday Blue Law" forbidding alcohol sales. One observer remarked that when "the parade marched past the reviewing stand carrying banners deriding Roosevelt . . . a marcher shouted loudly: 'Wo ist Roosevelt?' Grinning happily, Roosevelt leaned over the balustrade and shouted back: 'Hier bin ich!' . . . This brought a roar from the crowd and turned what had been intended as an attack on the Commissioner into a personal triumph . . . Roosevelt later on in his term gave even more display of his thereafter frequently proven aptitude for handling outbursts of German temperament, including those of Kaiser Wilhelm. As Police Commissioner, his opportunity was provided when an aggressively *anti*-Semitic orator, Rector Ahlwardt, arrived in New York, to give a lecture and required police protection. Jewish elements in the city promptly

retaliated that the pastor, far from receiving protection, be refused permission to speak at all. How Roosevelt solved this dilemma with characteristic aplomb, and in a way that made headlines in Europe, was engagingly narrated in his autobiography: 'The proper thing to do was to make him ridiculous. Accordingly, I detailed for his protection a Jewish Sergeant and a score or two of Jewish policemen. He made his harangue against the Jews under the active protection of some forty policemen, every one of them a Jew!" (Busch, 1963, pp. 97–98). Another adroit commentator was Dr. A. L. Wolbart (1898), Republican leader in the Fourth Assembly District. While replying to a letter from Roosevelt, he wrote: "With an honest and energetic and aggressive campaign the district will give you a handsome vote . . . The district is largely Jewish and can be depended on to support you heartily. You may have many friends among the downtown Jews, who have always admired an honest public official. As the campaign advances it would be well to interest the east side peddlers in a body in your own behalf. They will never forget the noble treatment received at your hands while in the Police Department" (p. 884). Long before Roosevelt had even announced any ambition to run for Governor "The *Ithaca Daily News* went a step further by declaring Roosevelt to be its candidate for the 1896 Republican nomination for President" (Busch, *op. cit.,* p. 99). It has been estimated that 15 Jewish sailors went down with the *U.S.S. Maine* on February 15, 1898. Many, eager to demonstrate gratitude to their new country, felt a subconscious urge to avenge wrongs that had formerly been inflicted upon a vast multitude of exiles and martyrs victimized by unforgotten Spanish executioners.

PART F

1. See data in *Cornell University* Library Archive #2009 ("The Florence Ledyard Cross Kitchelt Papers, 1874-1961") which contains a notebook complied by Florence Ledyard Cross (a former settlement worker and descendant of the *Civil War* era abolitionist Gerrit Smith) listing 186 citizen-youths who resided at the Freeville premises from 1896 through 1899 while she was a volunteer.

2. Commons warned *Syracuse University's* Chancellor James R. Day, during his abbreviated association as a Department of Sociology faculty-appointee, that he was a radical and a supporter of radical causes. The Chancellor reputedly said it was acceptable as long as he was not an "obnoxious Socialist." Commons did not think that he was "obnoxious" in his radicalism but the rest of the faculty apparently thought otherwise. He was dismissed because it was thought that his presence discouraged donors from making gifts to the University (Commons, 1963, pp. 53–54).

3. It was the custom of Thomas Mott Osborne (*i.e.,* an Auburn resident, Harvard graduate, international industrialist and life-long benefactor of the *Republic* who served both as an early member of its Board of Directors and President Directors and President of its first Executive Committee who was notably elected president of the *National Association of Junior Republics* at New York City in 1897 and later served as Warden of *Sing Sing Prison*) " . . . to wheel over the miles from Auburn to Freeville on his bicycle and arrive in a whirl of dust" according to his biographer (Chamberlain,

op. cit., p. 226) perhaps because of the intermittent schedules of the Lehigh Valley Railroad's Sayre-Auburn and Elmira-Cortland branch routes. Osborne's humanistic bent in becoming a nationally renowned prison reformer was perhaps influenced, in part, by his great-aunt, the suffragist Lucretia Coffin Mott. See also data in Syracuse University Special Collections Center Library (*The William Mott Osborne* Papers).

Appendix 1

"Daddy's Prophecy"

"One hundred years from now there will be a National Junior Republic to which all Junior Republics will belong. One point will be the Capitol. They will not be Junior Republics but Junior States. (A Jr. State in each State or perhaps two or three Jr. States in each State having counties formed). There will be a Republic in the Philippine Islands, Porto [sic] Cuba. And in all Republic countries, or something to correspond to the system of government of the county or country in which they are located. There will be no reform schools; no Homes with a capital H. Boarding schools, etc. will be sunk in Republics to a great degree. This will become a system of education for nearly every boy or girl. Wherever a republic is located—around that vicinity will be a community of graduates having some co-operation among themselves. These communities will be remarkable for the excellent local government. There will be former Jr. Republic citizens in the U. S. Senate, Congress (at the end of the 20th-century or before) and occupying governmental positions; men of wealth, scientists, inventors of the highest order. This will be death to pauperism. Citizens not gaining distinction will be known for their industry, self reliance and character" [See container 3, folder 17 of Cornell University Library Archive #800 ("*The William R. George Family Papers, 1750–1989*)].

Nota Bene: The above-quoted transcript was handwritten on New Year's evening just before midnight on December 31, 1899 while the speaker sat "at the end of the girl's sitting room by the window" with 19 signers gathered around. The sixth sentence seems to reflect "Daddy's" *anti*-regimental ardor then prevalent at reform schools, so-called "Homes" and boarding schools.

Appendix 2

October 9, 1899 letter from Richard Feinberg to William R. George

[in container 3, folder 15 of Cornell University Library Archive #800 (*"The William R. George Family Papers, 1750 –1989"***)]**

"I thought I would write you a short letter and let you know how I am getting on since I left the Rep[ublic]. I am well and in good health as I hope you and everyone else is in the G.J.R. [George Junior Republic]. Now Daddy to come down to business. I made a very costly mistake by leaving the Rep. But I am satisfied with one thing, and that is that it gave me a severe lesson of which I shall never forget. I don't like this place at all. I would not stay here under any circumstances, cause it aint the right place for me. I wish you would write a nice letter to my mother and tell what you think best for me. She is very angry at me cause I don't like it. In fact I don't blame her cause it is all my fault that I am placed in such circumstances but hereafter I will take advice of my elders first and my youngers next. My mother thinks this is a good place because there are all jews, but I can't get along with them. Not to run the jews down, but to tell the truth I was never among more noisy and uncivilized people than I am at the present. And if you write a nice letter to my mother I think it will be all right. I imagine that you will laugh yourself to death just to think how foolish I was in leaving you. Now Daddy tell me whether I can get a third rate ticket from Philadelphia to Freeville cause it will cost quite a little and you would save me about $6.00 or $7.00 which is quite a good deal for me now days. I am about 56 miles from Phil. It is a small place entirely settled by the jews. It contains 1,000 inhabitants. It is 10 miles from the ocean. I am very lonesome for the Republic and the boys as well. If I had to walk all the way home, I would much rather do it than stay here. I will tell you more about it some other time. Please tell me all about everything when you write. I will close now with love to all. I remain your friend [signed]."

Nota Bene: The letter writer's grammatical errors have not been disturbed. The original stationery upon which the above-quoted transcript was handwritten by the sender consists of four pages. Each sheet is imprinted at the top as follows: "The Baron de Hirsch Agricultural and Industrial School.

De Hirsch Hall" (centered upon four embossed lines); "Woodbine, N.J. ———, 189" (right margin); "H[irsch] L[eib] Sabsovich, Superintendent" (left margin) [*i.e.,* The bracketed insertions have been supplied by author for clarity. Other archival data discloses that several of the letter-writer's co-enrollees were state-subsidized orphans hailing from New Jersey and adjoining jurisdictions].

Appendix 3

Glossary

[Throughout the preceding text and *Appendixes 1* and *2,* French, German and Latin phrases, words and abbreviations have been italicized. Transliterated Hebrew and Yiddish phrases, words and abbreviations have likewise been italicized except for right-hand sided definitions in this appendix]

Kibbutz	a collective communal entity in Israel
Kosher	ritually pure
Jüdisch-Theologisches Seminar	a Jewish Theological Seminary
Yeshivot	educational institutions [singular = yeshiva] in eastern Europe for orthodox modes of religious studies
wissenschaft [abbreviated term]	19th-century Germanic-evolved concept envisioning scientific study of Jewish knowledge
Vilna Gaon	Elijah ben Solomon (1720-1797), a sage who resisted spread of Hasidism among Jews of Lithuania [Vilna = Lithuanian city] and Poland fearing that creation of such groups would weaken the Jewish community
Bar Mitzvah	male religious rite at age 13 upon entering adulthood
Adath Yeshurun	community of Israel [last word = poetic variant]
hazzan-shochet-mohel	religious official performing combined rites as cantor/reader of prayers/kosher butcher/circumciser

Appendix 3

mishpocha	extended family or relations
tumbler	jokester or life of the party
shul	congregation or place of worship
Chevra Chyateem	tailors' guild
Der Rabbiner	The Rabbi [male]
Landsmen	a fellow native of one's 'Old country'
Herr M	Mr. M
Chabad]	Hebrew acronym for the three intellectual faculties of wisdom, comprehension and knowledge
YIVO [acronym]	Institute for [Scientific = systematized knowledge as object of study] Yiddishist Studies
chutzpah	audacious behavior
Ashkenazi	Yiddish-speaking Jews with roots in eastern Europe
Deutsch	German
Frankfurter Allgemeine Zeitung	Daily newspaper in Frankfurt-am-Main in Germany
SYRAKUS	Syracuse
Svencionys	Lithuanian city
Vilkaviskus	Lithuanian city
Proskurov	Russian city
Litvaks	Jews whose heritage is traceable to former Grand Duchy of Lithuania
Frumah Packard Cemetery	Syracuse cemetery honoring local [first word = pious] woman founder
kleynshik pintele yud	tiny round dot diacritical vowel mark above tiniest Hebrew letter
yid	Jew [slang]
galut	exile
dos pintele yid	proverbial Yiddish phrase = a tiny dot
malchamovitz	angel of death
'Wo ist Roosevelt?'	Who is Roosevelt?
'Hier bin ich!'	Here am I!
Shayn farges'n	I've forgotten
Kiddush	ceremony proclaiming holiness of incoming Sabbath

Bibliography

Adler, C. (1931). *Louis Marshall: A Biographical Sketch.* New York, NY: The American Jewish Committee.
Adler, S. & Connolly, T. E. (1960). *From Ararat to Suburbia: The History of the Jewish Community of Buffalo.* Philadelphia, PA: Jewish Publication Society of America.
American Jewish Historical Society (2008). "Nathan Straus (1848–1931)." In: www.JewishVirtualLibrary.org
—— (2008). "Teddy Roosevelt: Jewish Avenger (1899)." In: www.JewishVirtualLibrary.org
Berkowitz, H. (1898). *Kiddush or Sabbath Sentiment in Home.* Philadelphia, PA: s.p. (*addendum*).
Bloom, H. (2008). "The Glories of Yiddish." In: *The New York Review of Books,* Vol. 55, No. 17, pp. 24–26.
Bondy, J. (1937). "Prelude." In: *The Pack Peddler.* Philadelphia, PA: John C. Winston Co.
Brickner, I. M. (1912). *The Jews of Rochester.* Rochester, NY: Historical Review Society.
Busch, N. E. (1963). *T.R.: The Story of Theodore Roosevelt.* New York, NY: Reynal & Co.
Chamberlain, R. W. (1935). *There Is No Truce: A Life of Thomas Mott Osborne.* New York, NY: The Macmillan Co.
Commons, J. R. (1897). "The Junior Republic, I." In: *The American Journal of Sociology,* Vol. 3, No. 3, pp. 281–296.
—— (1898). "The Junior Republic, II." In: *The American Journal of Sociology*, Vol. 3, No. 4, pp. 433–448.
—— (1963). *Myself, the Autobiography of John R. Commons.* Madison, WI: University of Wisconsin Press.
Crenson, M. A. (1998). *Building the Invisible Orphanage: A Pre-History of the American Welfare System.* Cambridge, MA: Harvard University Press.

Dobkowski, M. & Lovenheim, B. I. (1998). "Introduction: Beginning a Community." In: *A Family Among Families.* Rochester, NY: Jewish Home Foundation.

Elsner, H. L. (1890). *The Jewish Tidings* . May 2nd column, p. 1.

Falker, J. (1890). May 16th letter. In: *The Jewish Tidings*, p. 1.

Frederick, R. (2008). June 11th *Erie Times-News* column ("Chautauqua Jewish Groups Await New Home").

George, W. R. (1941). *Junior Republic Principals and Bulletins: A Series of Articles by William R. George, "Daddy," as he is known to boys and girls all over the world. These articles or "Bulletins" as Daddy is pleased to term them will explain clearly and definitely his ideas on this great educational movement of which he is the founder.* Freeville, NY: The George Junior Republic.

Ginsburg, L. M. (2001). *Israelites in Blue and Gray: Unchronicled Tales from Two Cities.* Lanham, MD: University Press of America.

Goldstein, H. (1966). *The Home on Gorham Street and the Voices of its Children.* Tuscaloosa, AL: University of Alabama Press.

Guttman, A. (1890). *The Jewish Tidings* . May 2nd column, p. 1.

——— 1891). April 3rd column quoting excerpted passage from lecture reprinted in *The Jewish Tidings* ("Dr. Guttman's Interesting Lectures"), p. 7.

——— (1893). October 27th column quoting excerpted passage from lecture reprinted in *The Jewish Tidings* ("Education"), p. 7.

Handlin, O. (1957). "Introduction." In: *Louis Marshall: Champion of Liberty,* Vol. I, C. Reznikoff, ed. Philadelphia, PA: Jewish Publication Society of America.

Jacobs, J. (1889). July 5th column ("A Bright Young Poetess"). In: *The Jewish Tidings*, p. 3.

——— 1889). November 20th column ("My Childhood"). In: *The Jewish Tidings*, p. 8.

——— 1890). April 25th column ("Poem on a Party"). In: *The Jewish Tidings*, p. 3.

Jabobson, N. (1890). *The Jewish Tidings* . May 2nd column, p. 1.

Karp, A. J. (1985). *Haven and Home: A History of Jews in America.* New York, NY: Schocken Books.

——— (1998). *Jewish Continuity in America: Creative Survival in a Free Society.* Tuscaloosa, AL: University of Alabama Press.

Kasdin, P. (2005). *The Future Begins with the Past: An Archives Exhibit of Jewish Rochester.* Rochester, NY: Fossil Press

Kohn, S. J. (1959). *The Jewish Community of Utica, New York: 1847–1948.* New York, NY: American Jewish Historical Society.

Korn, B. W. (1954). *Eventful Years and Experiences: Studies in Nineteenth Century American Jewish History.* Cincinnati, OH: The American Jewish Archives.

——— (1972). *German-Jewish Intellectual Influences on American Jewish Life, 1824–1972.* Syracuse, NY: Syracuse University Press.

Kris, E. (1956). *The Selected Papers of Ernst Kris.* New Haven, CT: Yale University Press.

Landsberg, M. (1890). August 15th letter to editor ("Rev. Dr. Landsberg's Reply to the *Tidings.*" In: *The Jewish Tidings*, p. 7.

Learsi, R. (1954). *The Jews in America: A History.* Cleveland, OH: The World Publishing Co.

Levy, S. D. (1900). *An Appeal on Behalf of the Hebrew Sheltering Society of New York Orphan Asylum.* New York, NY: Board of Management.

Lowenstein, S. (1932). "Dr. Lee K. Frankel, 1867–1931." In: *American Jewish Yearbook,* Vol. 34, pp. 121–140.

Marshall, L. (1890). *The Jewish Tidings* . May 2nd column, p. 1.

—— (1908). "Proceedings of the 5th National Conference of Jewish Charities." Baltimore, MD: Kohn & Pollock, Inc. (1909, pp. 112–122).

Munsterberg, H. (1902). "'Poor Relief in the United States:' A View of a German Expert." In: *American Journal of Sociology,* Vol. 7, pp. 659-696.

Peissackwotch, M. (n.d.). Unpublished Manuscript (pp. 746–747 & 750–751 translated by Ted Brodek of Atlanta, GA). In: *United States Territorial Collection (i.e.,* YIVO Archive #RG 117, Container 111). New York, NY.

'*Philologos*' *On Language* (2008). March 13th column ("Last Names, Lost in Translation"). In: www.Forward.com

—— March 27th column ("Myths and Facts"). In: www.Forward.com

Potok, C. (1967). *The Chosen.* New York, NY: Simon & Schuster.

Provol, W. L. (1937). *The Pack Peddler.* Philadelphia, PA: John C. Winston Co.

Reznicoff, C. (1957). *Louis Marshall: Champion of Liberty,* Vols. I & II. Philadelphia, PA: Jewish Publication Society of America.

Richardson, I. K. (1938). "A Study of Institutional and Foster Care for Dependent Children: Based Upon a Sample Survey of the Former Residents and Later Foster Home Placements of the *Jewish Orphan Asylum of Western New York.*" Rochester, NY: University of Rochester Master's Degree Thesis.

Rose, E. L. (1852). "Equal Rights for Women." In: *A Documentary History of the Jews in America: 1645–1875,* M. U. Schappes, ed. New York, NY: Schocken Books (1971), pp. 325–326.

Rosenberg, S. E. (1954). *The Jewish Community of Rochester, 1843–1925.* New York, NY: Columbia University Press.

Rosenstock, M. (1965). *Louis Marshall: Defender of Jewish Rights.* Detroit, MI: Wayne University Press.

Rudolph, B. G. (1970). *From a Minyan to a Community: A History of the Jews of Syracuse.* Syracuse, NY: Syracuse University Press.

Stolz, J. (1888). May 11th column reprinted in *The Jewish Tidings* ("Importance of Education"), p. 7.

The Jewish Tidings (1888). June 8th column, p. 2.

—— 1890). July 11th reprint of undated article published in *Rochester Sunday Times*, p. 8.

—— 1890). July 18th editorial, p. 4.

The William R. George Family Papers, 1750–1989. In: Cornell University Library Archive #800. Ithaca, NY.

The Florence Ledyard Cross Kitchelt Papers, 1874–1961. In: Cornell University Library Archive #2009. Ithaca, NY.

The William Mott Osborne Papers. In: Syracuse University Special Collections Center. Syracuse, NY.

Webster's Seventh New Collegiate Dictionary. Springfield, MA: Merriam Co.

Wise, J. W. (1928). "Louis Marshall." In: *Jews are Like That!* Freeport, NY: Books for Libraries Press (pp. 177–205).

Wolbarst, A. L. (1898). October 3rd letter to Theodore Roosevelt. In: *The Letters of Theodore Roosevelt, Vol. II*. E. E. Morison, ed. (1951). Cambridge, MA: Harvard University Press (p. 884, fn. 1 to letter #1084).

About the Author

Lawrence M. Ginsburg is a "rusticated" (*i.e.,* 19th-century slang for "retired") lawyer. He has written, among *non*-legal publications, "Israelites in Blue and Gray: Unchronicled Tales from Two Cities (*University Press of America*, 2001); the essay "'Happyville' Deconstructed: An Over-caricatured Landmark in Southern Jewish History" (*The South Carolina Review*, 2006). Other endeavors include more then two dozen psychoanalytically-oriented papers authored or co-authored by him which have appeared in journals published in North America, Europe and Israel. Several have been translated into French, German and Hebrew. The author's wife—Sybil A. Ginsburg, M.D. —who is affiliated with the *Emory University Psychoanalytic Institute* shares an interest in his scholarly pursuits.

OTHER OF AUTHOR'S PUBLICATIONS

Israelites in Blue and Gray: Unchronicled Tales from Two Cities (2001)

"'Happyville' Deconstructed: An Over-Caricatured Landmark in Southern Jewish History," *The South Carolina Review,* Vol. 39, No. 1 (2006)

www.ingramcontent.com/pod-product-compliance
Lightning Source LLC
Chambersburg PA
CBHW070304230426
43664CB00014B/2629